JN194212

Handy **Japanese** Conversations

Master Phrases through MANGA

FREE AUDIO

Learn Japanese with Tanaka san

Chapters

Chapter **5** More Conversational Phrases

Chapter **6** Help Phrases

Introduction

Have you ever thought something along the lines of:
"Wouldn't it be fun to chat with locals on my trip to Japan?"
"I've never studied Japanese for real, but I'd really love to give it a shot and start with some basic phrases!"
Then this book is just right for you.

I run a YouTube channel called "Learn Japanese with Tanaka san." The concept of it is "sushi characters that make learning Japanese fun." I've been creating content with illustrations and animations I personally made to share information about Japanese language and culture.

Reading comments and messages from the over 500,000 subscribers on my channel, I've noticed a common desire my viewers have is to engage with others using Japanese.

So, I thought to myself: "I want to put together a collection of conversational phrases that absolute beginners, or people who have never learned Japanese, can just use straight away!" Which is why I set out to make this book.

In this book, you can learn some commonly used everyday conversational phrases in Japanese through 4-panel comics, which makes the learning process fun. You don't have to wade deep into the grammar first; you can just learn the phrases and start putting them to use. I'll also share some aspects of Japanese culture and customs that you won't easily find in textbooks.

Using the phrases covered in this book, you'll be able to confidently order at cafes and enjoy shopping when you visit Japan. You'll even be able to engage in small talk and make friends with people you meet for the first time.

Are you ready to embark on a journey of discovering a new world, meeting new people, and exploring a new version of yourself through Japanese?

はじめに

「日本旅行のとき、現地の人と会話できたらどれだけ楽しいだろう？」

「日本語を学んだことがないけど、まずは簡単なフレーズを覚えて話してみたい！」

本書はこのような思いをお持ちの方にぴったりの本です。

私は YouTube チャンネル『Learn Japanese with Tanaka san』を運営しています。「寿司のキャラクターが楽しく日本語を教える」というコンセプトのもと、イラストやアニメーションを使って日本語や日本文化に関するコンテンツを発信してきました。

50 万人を超えるチャンネル登録者のみなさんからのコメントやメッセージを読んでいると、「日本語を使って人と交流したい」という思いが多くの方にあることがわかりました。

「日本語を学んだことがない方や、勉強し始めたばかりの初心者の方がすぐ使うことのできる会話フレーズ集を作りたい！」

そんな気持ちから本書を制作しました。

本書では、日常生活でよく使う日本語の会話フレーズを 4 コマ漫画で楽しみながら学ぶことができます。文法をまだよく知らなくても大丈夫。フレーズを丸ごと覚えて、今日から使い始めることができます。さらに、教科書ではなかなか知ることのできない日本の文化や習慣についても紹介しています。

本書で取り上げているフレーズを使えば、日本を訪れたときに自信を持ってカフェで注文したり、ショッピングを楽しんだりできるようになります。さらに、初めて会う人とちょっとした会話を交わしたり、仲良くなったりすることもできるようになるでしょう。

さぁ、日本語を通して、新しい世界・新しい人・新しい自分と出会う準備はできましたか？

Basics of Japanese

There are three types of characters in the Japanese writing system: "hiragana," "katakana," and "kanji."

Hiragana Hiragana is the most basic set of characters in the Japanese writing system, representing the basic sounds in the Japanese language. Each hiragana character corresponds to one syllable.

Katakana Very similar to hiragana, katakana is also a set of characters used to represent the sounds of the Japanese language. It is mostly used for writing loanwords from foreign languages and is also used when writing foreign names or foreign place names. Just like hiragana, each katakana character represents one syllable. Think of them sort of like hiragana in italics!

Kanji Kanji are characters that were originally taken from China. Unlike hiragana and katakana, each kanji character has its own meaning. There are a vast number of kanji characters, with over 2,000 of them being used in everyday life. It's also very common for a single kanji to have multiple readings.

Japanese sentences are constructed by combining hiragana, katakana, and kanji characters.

マイクさん、今日は いい 天気ですね。
Maiku san, kyoo wa ii tenki desu ne.
Mike-san, today's weather is nice, isn't it?

Since this book was made for Japanese beginners, most of it is written using hiragana; apart from some elementary-level kanji.

Romaji There is also *romaji*, which is short for roman *ji*, or roman characters. It is a system for representing the pronunciation of Japanese using the Latin alphabet. We also use it when typing Japanese on a computer keyboard. Once you learn the hiragana and katakana, it's a good idea to try to rely less on *romaji* and read in Japanese script as much as you can.

Hiragana and Katakana Charts

ひらがな
HIRAGANA

わ wa	ら ra	や ya	ま ma	は ha	な na	た ta	さ sa	か ka	あ a
	り ri		み mi	ひ hi	に ni	ち chi	し shi	き ki	い i
を o	る ru	ゆ yu	む mu	ふ fu	ぬ nu	つ tsu	す su	く ku	う u
	れ re		め me	へ he	ね ne	て te	せ se	け ke	え e
ん n	ろ ro	よ yo	も mo	ほ ho	の no	と to	そ so	こ ko	お o

りゃ rya	みゃ mya	ぴゃ pya	びゃ bya	ひゃ hya	にゃ nya	ぢゃ ja	ちゃ cha	じゃ ja	しゃ sha	ぎゃ gya	きゃ kya	ぱ pa	ば ba	だ da	ざ za	が ga
												ぴ pi	び bi	ぢ ji	じ ji	ぎ gi
りゅ ryu	みゅ myu	ぴゅ pyu	びゅ byu	ひゅ hyu	にゅ nyu	ぢゅ ju	ちゅ chu	じゅ ju	しゅ shu	ぎゅ gyu	きゅ kyu	ぷ pu	ぶ bu	づ zu	ず zu	ぐ gu
												ぺ pe	べ be	で de	ぜ ze	げ ge
りょ ryo	みょ myo	ぴょ pyo	びょ byo	ひょ hyo	にょ nyo	ぢょ jo	ちょ cho	じょ jo	しょ sho	ぎょ gyo	きょ kyo	ぽ po	ぼ bo	ど do	ぞ zo	ご go

カタカナ
KATAKANA

ワ wa	ラ ra	ヤ ya	マ ma	ハ ha	ナ na	タ ta	サ sa	カ ka	ア a
	リ ri		ミ mi	ヒ hi	ニ ni	チ chi	シ shi	キ ki	イ i
ヲ o	ル ru	ユ yu	ム mu	フ fu	ヌ nu	ツ tsu	ス su	ク ku	ウ u
	レ re		メ me	ヘ he	ネ ne	テ te	セ se	ケ ke	エ e
ン n	ロ ro	ヨ yo	モ mo	ホ ho	ノ no	ト to	ソ so	コ ko	オ o

リャ rya	ミャ mya	ピャ pya	ビャ bya	ヒャ hya	ニャ nya	ヂャ ja	チャ cha	ジャ ja	シャ sha	ギャ gya	キャ kya	パ pa	バ ba	ダ da	ザ za	ガ ga
												ピ pi	ビ bi	ヂ ji	ジ ji	ギ gi
リュ ryu	ミュ myu	ピュ pyu	ビュ byu	ヒュ hyu	ニュ nyu	ヂュ ju	チュ chu	ジュ ju	シュ shu	ギュ gyu	キュ kyu	プ pu	ブ bu	ヅ zu	ズ zu	グ gu
												ペ pe	ベ be	デ de	ゼ ze	ゲ ge
リョ ryo	ミョ myo	ピョ pyo	ビョ byo	ヒョ hyo	ニョ nyo	ヂョ jo	チョ cho	ジョ jo	ショ sho	ギョ gyo	キョ kyo	ポ po	ボ bo	ド do	ゾ zo	ゴ go

Map of Japan

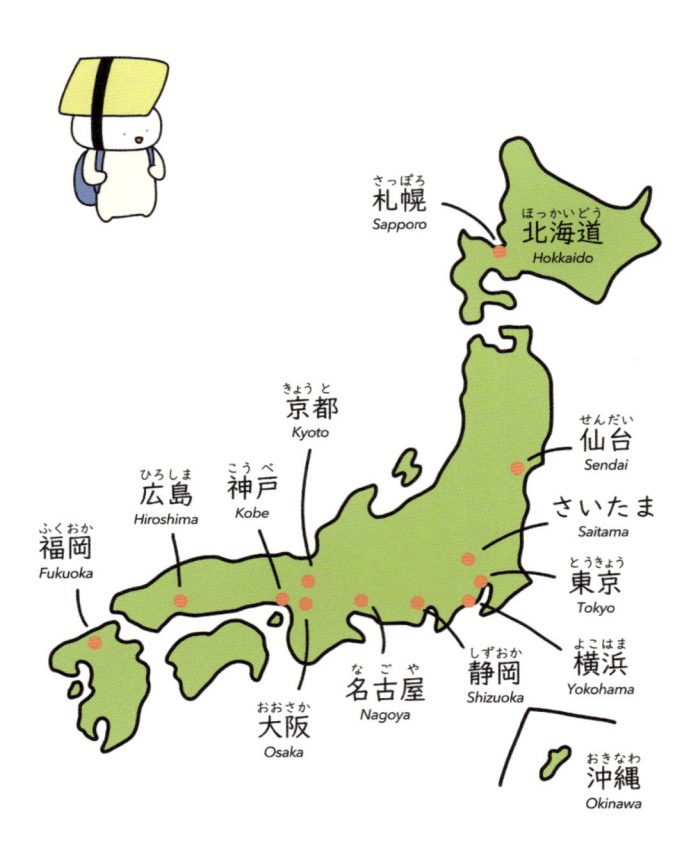

札幌 (さっぽろ) Sapporo
北海道 (ほっかいどう) Hokkaido
京都 (きょうと) Kyoto
仙台 (せんだい) Sendai
広島 (ひろしま) Hiroshima
神戸 (こうべ) Kobe
さいたま Saitama
福岡 (ふくおか) Fukuoka
東京 (とうきょう) Tokyo
横浜 (よこはま) Yokohama
大阪 (おおさか) Osaka
名古屋 (なごや) Nagoya
静岡 (しずおか) Shizuoka
沖縄 (おきなわ) Okinawa

How to Use This Book

1. Phrase
2. Audio track number
3. 4-Panel comic utilizing the phrase
4. Explanation of the phrase
5. Examples of conversations using the phrase (Try reading them aloud!)
6. Additional phrases and vocabulary
7. Some useful trivia about Japanese culture and customs

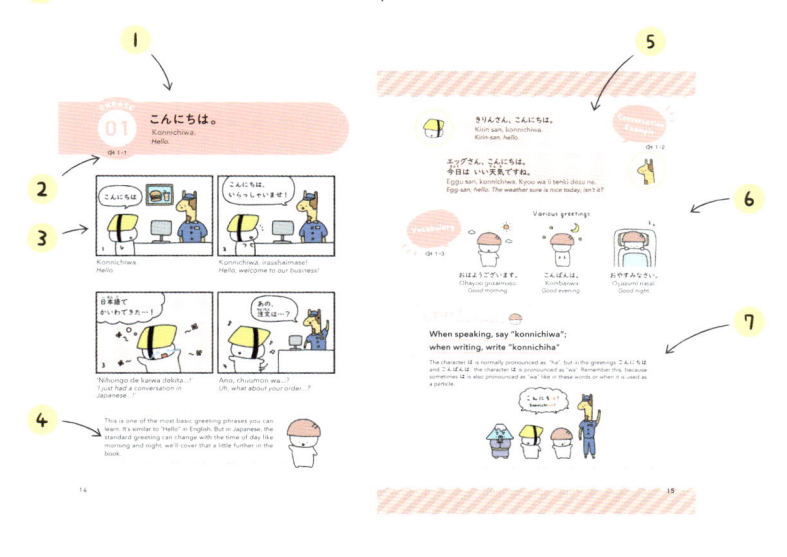

Listening to the Audio

You can download the audio package by scanning the code below.

Characters' Introduction

Tanaka-san

Is a piece of tuna sushi.
Teaches Japanese.
Likes coffee.

Egg-san

Is a piece of *tamago* sushi.
Studies Japanese.
Likes Tofu-san.

Tofu-san

Friend of Tanaka-san and Egg-san. Possesses a mysterious charm and beauty.

Kirin-san

Works a variety of part-time jobs to fulfill his dream of becoming a singer.

Fuji-san

Old man who lives near Tanaka-san's house.

Takoyaki-san

Originally from Osaka.
Owns and runs a *takoyaki* shop.

Tempura-san

A waiter at a cafe who secretly has feelings for Tofu-san.

Ichigo-chan

A popular idol. Tanaka-san is her biggest fan.

Chapter

1

Basic Phrases

こんにちは。

Konnichiwa.
Hello.

◁)) 1-1

Konnichiwa.
Hello.

Konnichiwa, irasshaimase!
Hello, welcome to our business!

'Nihongo de kaiwa dekita...!'
'I just had a conversation in Japanese...!'

Ano, chuumon wa...?
Uh, what about your order...?

This is one of the most basic greeting phrases you can learn. It's similar to "Hello" in English. But in Japanese, the standard greeting can change with the time of day like morning and night, we'll cover that a little further in the book.

きりんさん、こんにちは。
Kirin san, konnichiwa.
Kirin-san, hello.

🔊 1-2

エッグさん、こんにちは。
今日は いい 天気ですね。
（きょう）（てん き）
Eggu san, konnichiwa. Kyoo wa ii tenki desu ne.
Egg-san, hello. The weather sure is nice today, isn't it?

Various greetings

🔊 1-3

おはようございます。
Ohayoo gozaimasu.
Good morning.

こんばんは。
Kombanwa.
Good evening.

おやすみなさい。
Oyasumi nasai.
Good night.

\ Tips / from Tanaka

When speaking, say "konnichiwa"; when writing, write "konnichiha"

The character は is normally pronounced as "ha," but in the greetings こんにちは and こんばんは, the character は is pronounced as "wa." Remember this, because sometimes は is also pronounced as "wa" like in these words or when it is used as a particle.

ありがとうございます。

Arigatoo gozaimasu.

Thank you.

🔊 2-1

Ano...
Uh...

Hankachi otoshimashita yo.
You dropped your handkerchief.

A...! Arigatoo gozaimasu!
Oh, thank you!

Kondo wa sumaho
otoshimashita yo...!
Now you dropped your phone...!

This is a phrase that expresses gratitude. You might already be familiar with the word ありがとう, which is used in close relationships like with family or friends. ありがとうございます is the formal form. It's common to use ありがとうございます when expressing gratitude to strangers or service staff.

さいふ おとしましたよ。
Saifu otoshimashita yo.
You dropped your wallet.

Conversation Example

🔊 2-2

ありがとうございます。
Arigatoo gozaimasu.
Thank you.

いえいえ。
Ieie.
No problem.

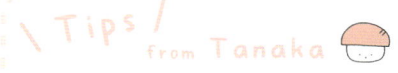
\ Tips / from Tanaka

What to say when you hear ありがとうございます ?

When someone says ありがとうございます , how should you respond? In many Japanese textbooks they like to suggest the following phrase:

どういたしまして。 Doo itashimashite. *You're welcome.*

While this phrase is indeed used in some situations, it's also quite formal. In actual daily life, it's more common to say:

いえいえ。 Ieie. *No problem.*

Sometimes, you can respond by just smiling or nodding without saying anything at all. Try to pay attention to how others react when you say ありがとうございます . You'll start to get a sense of how to reply.

すみません。

Sumimasen.
Excuse me.

🔊 3-1

'Uuun...'
'Hmm...'

Sumimasen.
Excuse me.

Eki wa doko desu ka?
Where is the station?

Sumimasen... Motto yukkuri...
Sorry, could you slow that down...?

This is a phrase that is used daily. **すみません** can be pronounced as **すいません** (suimasen) and can be used when apologizing, asking questions or when making requests. The phrase can also be used as an expression of gratitude, as an alternative to **ありがとうございます** but implies a sense of apology for not being able to do something in return when someone has done something for you.

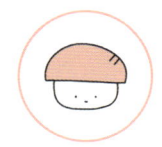

すみません、
ちずは ありますか？

Sumimasen, chizu wa arimasu ka?
Excuse me, do you have a map?

🔊 3-2

はい、どうぞ。

Hai, doozo.
Yeah, here.

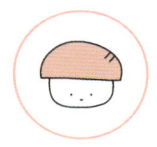

ありがとうございます。

Arigatoo gozaimasu.
Thank you.

Tips from Tanaka

Various expressions of apology

There are many other words for apologizing besides すみません in Japanese. In practice, it's completely okay to just stick with すみません when you need to apologize, but you might also hear the following expressions:

Casual

わるいね。 Waruine. *My bad.*

ごめん。 Gomen. *Sorry.*

ごめんなさい。 Gomen nasai. *I'm sorry.*

すみません。 Sumimasen. *Apologies.*

もうしわけございません。 Mooshiwake gozaimasen. *I apologize.*

Formal

はい。／いいえ。

Hai. / Iie.

Yes. / No.

Eggu san, imasu ka?
Is Egg-san here?

Hai!
Yes!

Shukudai wa shimashita ka?
Did you do your homework?

Iie...
No...

はい is not just simply translated to "Yes"; it's also used as an affirmative response similar to "uh-huh" in English. Additionally, in Japan, nodding the head up and down indicates agreement or affirmation, while shaking the head side to side indicates disagreement or negation.

きょうかしょは ありますか？

Kyookasho wa arimasu ka?

Do you have your textbook?

 Conversation Example

◁)) 4-2

はい、あります。

Hai, arimasu.

Yes, I do.

１２ページを 見てください。

Juuni peeji o mite kudasai.

Please turn to page 12 then.

 \Tips/ from Tanaka

Cultural aspects of nodding and shaking thehead

「はい…はい… (hai ... hai...)」

If you've conversed with Japanese people before, you might have noticed how often they nod and verbally affirm during a conversation.

In Japan, nodding and affirming verbally are considered important for indicating understanding or agreement with the speaker's statements. It's a way of showing, "I'm listening to what you're saying."

For those from cultures where nods and affirmatives are less common, it might seem like an interruption to their own speech.
However, being aware of this cultural aspect in Japan can be quite helpful.

はい…
はい…

05 おねがいします。

Onegai shimasu.
Please.

🔊 5-1

Fukuro goriyoo desu ka?
Do you need a bag?

Hai, onegai shimasu!
Yes, please!

Ichi mai go en desu ga...
It costs 5 yen per bag.

Yappari daijoobu desu!
On second thought, I'm fine!

This phrase comes in handy when you need or request something from someone. It's a polite way to communicate your needs, which can help maintain smooth interpersonal relationships. You'll often hear it used at convenience stores when you want to ask for a bag or chopsticks, as seen in the comic above.

おはし ごりようですか？
Ohashi goriyoo desu ka?
Do you need chopsticks?

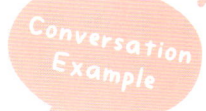
Conversation Example

🔊 5-2

はい、おねがいします。ありがとうございます。
Hai, onegai shimasu. Arigatoo gozaimasu.
Yes, please. Thank you.

Frequently asked questions at convenience stores

Bonus Phrases

🔊 5-3

おはし
ごりようですか？
Ohashi
goriyoo desu ka?
Do you need chopsticks?

あたためますか？
Atatamemasu ka?
Do you want this heated up?

レジぶくろ
ごりようですか？
Rejibukuro
goriyoo desu ka?
Do you need a bag?

How to answer

はい、おねがいします。
Hai, onegai shimasu.
Yes, please.
(when you want it)

いいえ、だいじょうぶです。
Iie, daijoobu desu.
No, I'm fine.
(when you don't want it)

Tips from Tanaka

よろしく おねがいします Yoroshiku onegai shimasu

よろしく おねがいします is a very commonly used fixed phrase in Japanese that incorporates the term おねがいします.

This phrase has a similar use as おねがいします. It's mostly used during self-introductions, and implies "I hope we can get along" or "I hope we can build a good relationship," when meeting someone for the first time. Try saying this phrase when introducing yourself to someone.
For example:

田中です。よろしく おねがいします。
Tanaka desu. Yoroshiku onegai shimasu.
I'm Tanaka. Nice to meet you.

わかりました。

Wakarimashita.
Understood.

🔊 6-1

Sumimasen, Oosaka eki wa doko desu ka?
Excuse me, where is Osaka Station?

Hidari ni itte kudasai.
Try heading left and you'll see it.

Wakarimashita.
Arigatoo gozaimasu!
Understood. Thank you!

Socchi wa migi desu yo...!
That's your right...!

This is a phrase you use when you want to communicate that you understood what the other person said. In conversation, it's sometimes crucial to clearly communicate whether you understood something or not. While replying with a simple はい from Phrase 4 might suffice, it could also leave the other person wondering, "Did they really understand me just now?" If you want to explicitly communicate that you understood what the other person said, try replying with a confident, わかりました.

明日、8時に ここに きてください。
Ashita, hachi ji ni koko ni kite kudasai.
Please be here tomorrow at 8 o'clock.

Conversation Example

🔊 6-2

はい、わかりました。
Hai, wakarimashita.
Okay, understood.

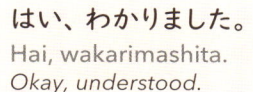

Bonus Phrases

Phrases to use when you don't understand the conversation

🔊 6-3

わかりません。
Wakarimasen.
I didn't understand that.

もういちど
おねがいします。
Moo ichido
onegai shimasu.
Could you say that again for me?

\ Tips / from Tanaka

Let's make use of すみません

When you don't understand the conversation, you can use the phrases introduced above to convey that you didn't understand or to ask for clarification. However, simply saying わかりません might come off as a bit too blunt. We can soften the tone a bit by adding すみません before the sentence to give it a more a polite impression.

すみません、わかりません。
Sumimasen, wakarimasen.
Sorry, I didn't understand that.

すみません、もういちど おねがいします。
Sumimasen, moo ichido onegai shimasu.
Sorry, could you please say that again?

すみません、もっと ゆっくり おねがいします。
Sumimasen, motto yukkuri onegai shimasu.
Sorry, could you please say that again slower?

わたしは ○○です。

Watashi wa ○○ desu.

I'm (name).

◁» 7-1

Watashi wa Tanaka desu.
I'm Tanaka.

Watashi wa nihonjin desu.
I'm Japanese.

Sorekara...
Watashi wa ninja desu.
And... I'm a ninja.

Kyoo wa harowin ja nai desu yo?
It's not Halloween today, you know?

This is a basic phrase that is used when talking about oneself. Those who enjoy manga or anime might already know that in Japanese, there are numerous ways to say "I." Besides わたし, there is あたし(atashi), ぼく (boku), おれ(ore), and many more. Which one you use depends on your gender and your relationship with the listener. わたし is a very commonly used general purpose first-person pronoun that can be used in any situation without issue, so it's a good idea to start with this one.

田中さんですか？
Tanaka san desu ka?
Are you Tanaka-san?

🔊 7-2

いいえ、わたしは エッグです。
Iie, watashi wa Eggu desu.
No, I'm Egg.

Phrase Practice

Let's try saying the below sentence
with the following words inside the parentheses.

わたしは （　　　）です。
Watashi wa (　　　) desu.
I'm (　　　).

🔊 7-3

ジョン	アメリカ人	タイ人
Jon	amerikajin	taijin
John	*American*	*Thai*

Tips from Tanaka

Japanese name order

In many Western countries, it's common to write names in the order of given name followed by surname, but in Japan, it's written surname first followed by a given name.

For example: 田中 太郎 (Tanaka Taroo)
surname　given name

When meeting someone for the first time or with people you're not very familiar with, it's common to add さん (san) after their surname when addressing them. It's considered rude not to use さん, so please be mindful of this.

It's said that Japan has around 100,000 different surnames. Some of the most common surnames nationwide include 佐藤 (Satoo), 鈴木 (Suzuki), and 高橋 (Takahashi). Have you heard any of these before? And by the way, 田中 is also a very common surname!

○○から きました。

○○ kara kimashita.
I'm from (place).

クロワッサンさんは
どこからきましたか？

Kurowassan san wa doko kara
kimashita ka?
Croissant-san, where are you from?

フランスから
きました

Furansu kara kimashita.
I'm from France.

フランスはとても
いいところですよ

たべものも
おいしいです

Furansu wa totemo ii tokoro desu
yo. Tabemono mo oishii desu.
France is such a nice place.
We have lots of good food.

ちょっと
ホームシックです

Chotto hoomushikku desu.
I miss my country a bit.

This phrase is used to tell others where you're from. You fill in the blank space of ○○から きました with the name of you are from. For instance, you can say フランスから きました by inserting the country's name, or パリ (Pari, Paris)から きました by adding the city's name. Japanese people you meet will likely be interested to hear where you're from. It's a great chance to share about your local area, including famous places, foods, and culture.

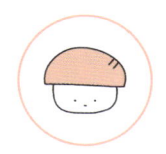

どこから きましたか？

Doko kara kimashita ka?

Where are you from?

🔊 8-2

フィリピンから きました。

Firipin kara kimashita.

I'm from the Philippines.

Phrase Practice

Let's try saying the below sentence with the following words inside the parentheses.

🔊 8-3

（　　　　）から きました。

（　　　　）kara kimashita.

I'm from (　　　　).

カナダ	イタリア	ベトナム	インドネシア
Kanada	Itaria	Betonamu	Indoneshia
Canada	*Italy*	*Vietnam*	*Indonesia*

\ Tips / from Tanaka

Phrases for when being asked questions

When asked where you're from, you might hear the following questions:

どこから きましたか？

Doko kara kimashita ka?

Where are you from?

Or you might be asked:

お国<ruby>国<rt>くに</rt></ruby>は どちらですか？

Okuni wa dochira desu ka?

Which country are you from?

ご出身<rt>しゅっしん</rt>は どちらですか？

Goshusshin wa dochira desu ka?

Which country did you come from?

Both どこ and どちら are used to mean "where." どちら sounds more polite. When you hear these phrases, respond with 〇〇から きました。

日本語を べんきょうしています。

Nihongo o benkyoo shite imasu.

I'm studying Japanese.

🔊 9-1

Eggu san wa nihongo ga joozu desu ne.
Egg-san, your Japanese is very good.

Mainichi nihongo o benkyoo shite imasu.
I study Japanese every day.

Doo yatte benkyoo shite imasu ka?
How do you study?

Mainichi anime o go jikan mite imasu.
I watch anime 5 hours a day.

This phrase can be used to convey that you are currently learning Japanese. People who don't know that you're studying Japanese might initially speak to you in English. Even if you can only speak a little Japanese, muster up the courage to let them know that you're in the process of learning Japanese. It's heartening for Japanese people to see foreigners putting effort into learning their language.

日本語を はなせますか？

Nihongo o hanasemasu ka?

Can you speak Japanese?

Conversation Example

🔊 9-2

はい、きょねんから 日本語を
べんきょうしています。

Hai, kyonen kara nihongo o benkyoo shite imasu.

Yes, I've been studying Japanese since last year.

Bonus Phrases

🔊 9-3

Tell them you can speak Japanese

日本語を
はなせます。

Nihongo o
hanase masu.

I can speak Japanese.

日本語を すこし
はなせます。

Nihongo o sukoshi
hanase masu.

*I can speak
a little bit of Japanese.*

＼Tips／ from Tanaka 🍄

How to respond when you're told "Your Japanese is good!"

Have you ever been unsure how to respond when someone says "Your Japanese is good!" even though you've only spoken a little Japanese? In such situations, there's a commonly used phrase that serves as a scripted response:

いいえ、まだまだです。

Iie, madamada desu.

No, I still have a long way to go.

In Japan, people try to maintain a sense of humility. Using the above phrase might help the conversation flow a bit better as it acknowledges you're aware there's room for improvement. However, there's no need to be too modest. If someone praises you, it's perfectly fine to simply say, ありがとうございます。

わたしは　学生です。

Watashi wa gakusee desu.

I'm a student.

Chiketto o misete kudasai.
Please show me your ticket.

Ano... Kore wa gakusee chiketto desu ga...
Um... This is a student ticket...

Watashi wa gakusee desu.
I'm a student.

'"Tempura udon daigaku"...?'
'Tempura Udon Noodle College...?'

The phrase わたしは　〇〇です introduced earlier in Phrase 7 can be used to state your affiliation or occupation. Sharing what you do and where you do it can help you connect with others. In the following sections, you'll find some different ways to express your affiliations and occupations, so feel free to practice using them.

エッグさんは かいしゃいんですか？

Eggu san wa kaishain desu ka?

Egg-san, are you employed?

いいえ、わたしは 学生です。
きりんさんも 学生ですか？

Iie, watashi wa gakusee desu.
Kirin san mo gakusee desu ka?

No, I'm a student. Kirin-san, are you a student too?

はい、大学生です。

Hai, daigakusee desu.

Yes, I'm a college student.

Let's try saying the below sentence with the following words inside the parentheses.

わたしは （　　　　） です。

Watashi wa (　　　) desu.

I'm (　　).

🔊 10-3

こうこうせい	大学生	かいしゃいん	きょうし
kookoosee	daigakusee	kaishain	kyooshi
high school student	*college student*	*company employee*	*teacher*

かんごし	デザイナー	エンジニア
kangoshi	dezainaa	enjinia
nurse	*designer*	*engineer*

\ Tips / from Tanaka

You can also use it to express where you work, like so,

〇〇で はたらいています。〇〇 de hataraite imasu. *I work at (place).*

For example:

スーパーで はたらいています。
Suupaa de hataraite imasu.
I work at a supermarket.

コンビニで はたらいています。
Kombini de hataraite imasu.
I work at a convenience store.

ラーメンが すきです。

Raamen ga suki desu.

I like ramen.

Watashi wa raamen ga suki desu.
I like ramen.

Watashi mo suki desu.
Me, too.

Jaa ima kara tabe ni ikimasen ka?
Well then why don't we go eat some now?

Ima wa chotto isogashii desu.
Right now I'm a little busy.

This phrase is used to express your favorite things. In ◯◯ が すきです (◯◯ ga suki desu, *I like (stuff you like)*), you can fill in the "◯◯" with the name of your favorite food, music, actor, manga or anime, YouTube channel, or anything else you like. Having friends to share your favorite things with will make your stay and life in Japan even more enjoyable.

まんがは なにが すきですか？
Manga wa nani ga suki desu ka?
What manga do you like?

Conversation Example

🔊 11-2

ワンピースが すきです。
Wampiisu ga suki desu.
I like ONE PIECE.

わたしも すきです！
Watashi mo suki desu!
Me, too!

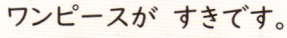

Phrase Practice

Let's try saying the below sentence
with the following words inside the parentheses.

（　　　）が すきです。
（　　　）ga suki desu.
I like (　　).

🔊 11-3

アニメ
anime
anime

サッカー
sakkaa
soccer

おこのみやき
okonomiyaki
okonomiyaki

 \ Tips / from Tanaka

Let's talk about likes and dislikes

Use the following phrases to express just how much you like or dislike something:

Like

だいすきです。 Daisuki desu. *I love it.*

すきです。 Suki desu. *I like it.*

あまり すきじゃ ないです。 Amari suki ja nai desu. *I don't really like it.*

きらいです。 Kirai desu. *I hate it.*

だいきらいです。 Daikirai desu. *I really hate it.*

Dislike

Let's Introduce Yourself

Let's combine the phrases learned in Chapter 1 to introduce yourself.

Self-introduction text

はじめまして。
Hajimemashite.
Nice to meet you.

○○から きました。
○○ kara kimashita.
I'm from (place).

よろしく おねがいします。
Yoroshiku onegai shimasu.
I hope we can get along.

わたしは ○○です。
Watashi wa ○○ desu.
My name is (name).

○○が すきです。
○○ ga suki desu.
I like (stuff you like).

Example 1

はじめまして。
Hajimemashite.
Nice to meet you.

わたしは クロワッサンです。
Watashi wa Kurowassan desu.
My name is Croissant.

フランスから きました。
Furansu kara kimashita.
I'm from France.

ショッピングが すきです。
Shoppingu ga suki desu.
I like shopping.

よろしく おねがいします。
Yoroshiku onegai shimasu.
I hope we can get along.

Example 2

はじめまして。
Hajimemashite.
Nice to meet you.

わたしは たこやきです。
Watashi wa Takoyaki desu.
My name is Takoyaki.

大阪（おおさか）から きました。
Oosaka kara kimashita.
I'm from Osaka.

おこのみやきが すきです。
Okonomiyaki ga suki desu.
I like okonomiyaki.

よろしく おねがいします。
Yoroshiku onegai shimasu.
I hope we can get along.

Chapter

2

Eating and Drinking Phrases

２人です。

ふたり

Futari desu.

Two of us.

Irasshaimase!
Nammee sama desu ka?
Welcome to our business!
How many in your party?

Futari desu.
Two of us.
Sannin desu.
Three of us.

Futari desu yo.
There's two.

Tanaka san no ushiro ni obake
ga imasu.
What about the ghost behind you?

This is a phrase for communicating how many people there are. When you enter a restaurant, you'll often be asked, なんめいさまですか？ It's helpful to show the number on your fingers so the staff can understand easily. By the way, in Japan, there are many restaurants where it's normal to dine alone. I'd encourage you to be brave and try out lots of places, even if you're alone, so you can enjoy some delicious food!

いらっしゃいませ。
なんめいさまですか？

Irasshaimase. Nammee sama desu ka?
Welcome to our business. How many in your party?

🔊 12-2

１人です。

Hitori desu.
Just one.

おすきな せきに どうぞ。

Osukina seki ni doozo.
Okay, feel free to seat yourself anywhere.

Counting the number of people

🔊 12-3

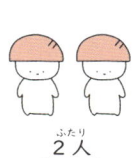
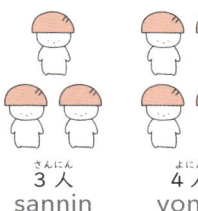
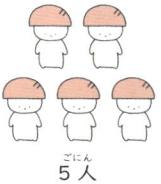

１人	２人	３人	４人	５人
hitori	futari	sannin	yonin	gonin
one person	*two people*	*three people*	*four people*	*five people*

When counting the number of people, we use the unit 人 (nin). However, 1人 (hitori) and 2人 (futari) are exceptions, so be careful.

\ Tips /
from Tanaka

Counting with fingers

In Japan, when counting numbers, it's common to use fingers as illustrated below.

1	2	3	4	5

注文 いいですか？

Chuumon ii desu ka?

Can we place our order?

🔊 13-1

Sumimasen, chuumon ii desu ka?
Excuse me, can we place our order?

Hambaagu ranchi setto hitotu.
I'll have the hamburger steak lunch set.
Watashi wa, etto...
Well, for me...

Yukkuri kimete kudasai.
Take your time.

Juu, kyuu, hachi...
10, 9, 8...

This phrase is used when you want to place an order. In some restaurants overseas, you may be used to having an assigned server, but in Japan, you can ask anyone. Once you have decided on your order, simply say すみません to signal a nearby staff member, then ask, 注文 いいですか？ to let them know you are ready to place your order.

すみません、
注文 いいですか？
Sumimasen, chuumon ii desu ka?
Excuse me, can I place my order?

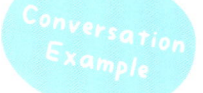

🔊 13-2

はい、おうかがいします。
Hai, oukagai shimasu.
Sure, what can I get you?

とんかつていしょく おねがいします。
Tonkatsu teeshoku onegai shimasu.
I'd like the tonkatsu set please.

かしこまりました。
Kashikomarimashita.
Very well.

\ Tips / from Tanaka

How to call the staff

If you want to call a server at a restaurant, simply say すみません to the nearest staff member. In smaller restaurants, you can also make eye contact them and slightly raise your hand. In chain restaurants such as "family restaurants," there is often a button on one of the tables that you can press to call for assistance.

これは なんですか?

Kore wa nan desu ka?
What's this?

Sumimasen.
Excuse me.

Kore wa nan desu ka?
What's this?

Saa... Nan de shoo.
Huh... I wonder myself.

Chuumon sure ba wakarimasu yo.
I guess if you order it you'll find out.

This phrase is used to ask about unfamiliar things, what they are, or what they are called. これ means "this" and refers to something in front of you. In Japan you will likely encounter new foods at restaurants or unusual products at stores for the first time. If you find something interesting, try using this phrase to ask about it directly.

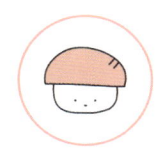

「からあげ」…? これは なんですか?
"Karaage"...? Kore wa nan desu ka?
"Karaage"...? What's this?

◁)) 14-2

フライドチキンです。
Furaidochikin desu.
It's fried chicken.

じゃあ、これに します。
Jaa, kore ni shimasu.
Then I'll have this.

Kore, Sore, Are

The これ in これは なんですか? changes depending on where the object is located relative to the speaker and the listener.

◁)) 14-3

これは なんですか?
Kore wa nan desu ka?
What's this?

それは なんですか?
Sore wa nan desu ka?
What's that?

あれは なんですか?
Are wa nan desu ka?
What's that over there?

\ Tips / from Tanaka

Strange foods in Japan

I'll introduce some slightly unusual foods in Japan that will make you want to ask, これは なんですか?

Their flavors are unique, and they may not be to everyone's taste, but don't knock it 'till you try it! If you have the chance, please give them a try at least once.

なっとう nattoo
fermented soybeans

うめぼし umeboshi
salt-pickled and dried Japanese plums

とろろ tororo
grated yam or Japanese mountain yam

ぶたにくは たべられません。

Butaniku wa taberaremasen.

I can't eat pork.

Butaniku wa taberaremasen.
I can't eat pork.

Kochira no menyuu wa butaniku ga haitte imasen yo.
The dishes on this part of the menu do not use pork.

Zembu oishisoo desu ne!
They all look so good!

Sanjuppun go
30 MINUTES LATER
'Mada desu ka...?'
'Still not ready to order...?'

This is a phrase used to describe what foods you cannot eat. If you have dietary restrictions due to allergies, being vegetarian, religious reasons or other personal reasons, it's important to remember this phrase. While there has been an increase in shops offering halal and vegan foods in the heavy urban areas of Japan in recent years, they are still relatively few in number. Even menus that may not seem to contain meat or fish could still use ingredients like broth or seasonings that you can't eat. If you have dietary restrictions, be sure to inform the staff before placing your order.

すしを たべに 行きませんか？

Sushi o tabe ni ikimasen ka?

Would you like to go have sushi together?

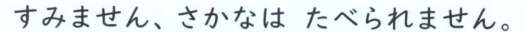

🔊 15-2

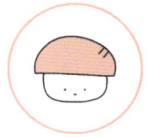

すみません、さかなは たべられません。

Sumimasen, sakana wa taberaremasen.

I'm sorry, but I can't eat fish.

じゃあ ヴィーガンレストランに 行きましょう。

Jaa viigan resutoran ni ikimashoo.

Oh, then how about a vegan restaurant?

Phrases to explain foods or drinks that you cannot consume

🔊 15-3

たまごは たべられません。	おさけは のめません。	ナッツアレルギー です。
Tamago wa taberaremasen.	Osake wa nomemasen.	Nattsu arerugii desu.
I can't eat eggs.	*I can't drink.*	*I'm allergic to nuts.*

\ Tips / from Tanaka

When expressing you don't prefer a food

If you want to express that you're not a big fan of something, but it's not due to allergies or religious reasons and you'd just rather not eat it if possible, you can use the following phrase:

○○は にがてです。 ○○ wa nigate desu.

I have a distaste for (food).

However, this might be too direct, and depending on how you say it, it could even hurt the other person's feelings. By adding すみません or ちょっと (chotto, *a bit*), you can soften your expression:

すみません、なっとうは ちょっと にがてです。

Sumimasen, nattoo wa chotto nigate desu.

Sorry, but I have a bit of distaste for natto.

すみません、のりは ちょっと にがてです。

Sumimasen, nori wa chotto nigate desu.

Sorry, but I have a bit of distaste for seaweed.

おすすめは なんですか？

Osusume wa nan desu ka?

What's your recommendation?

Osusume wa nan desu ka?
What's your recommendation?

Okyakusama ni wa kore ga
osusume desu.
I'd recommend this meal.

Watashi kodomo ja nai desu.
I'm not a kid.

おすすめ translates to "recommendation." For instance, when you're undecided about what to order at a restaurant, you can use this phrase to ask what dishes are popular at the restaurant or for the personal recommendations of the staff. It's not just a useful phrase for food but also for asking for recommendations for many things such as music, movies, and tourist spots.

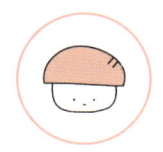

おすすめは なんですか？

Osusume wa nan desu ka?

What's your recommendation?

Conversation Example

🔊 16-2

とんかつが おすすめです。

Tonkatsu ga osusume desu.

I recommend the tonkatsu.

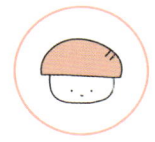

じゃあ とんかつ 一つ おねがいします。

Jaa tonkatsu hitotsu onegai shimasu.

Okay, can I get one order of tonkatsu?

\ Tips / from Tanaka

Share your recommendations as well

You don't have to only ask for recommendations, you can also share your own favorites and introduce them to others. It's a great way to share what you love with others!

〇〇が おすすめです。

〇〇 ga osusume desu.

I recommend (something).

For example:

アニメは ドラゴンボールが おすすめです。

Anime wa doragombooru ga osusume desu.

For anime, DRAGON BALL is my recommendation.

ラーメンは 『田中ラーメン』が おすすめです。

Raamen wa 『Tanaka raamen』 ga osusume desu.

For ramen, "Tanaka Ramen Shop" is my recommendation.

いただきます。

Itadakimasu.
Thank you for the meal. (before eating)

Waai! Hayaku tabemashoo!
Woo, let's dig in!

Chotto matte kudasai!
Hold on a second!

Nanika wasurete imasen ka?
Aren't you forgetting something?

Itadakimasu!
Thank you for the meal.

This is a phrase said before a meal. It expresses gratitude for the food itself and for the person who prepared it. In Japan, children are taught from a young age, both at home and in school, to say いただきます before eating. When eating school lunches, for example, everyone places their hands together in front of their faces and says いただきます in unison before starting to eat. By using this phrase before a meal, you might impress those around you as someone familiar with Japanese culture.

いただきます。
Itadakimasu.
Thank you for the meal.

◁») 17-2

どうぞ、たくさん たべてください。
Doozo, takusan tabete kudasai.
Please, eat all you want.

\ Tips / from Tanaka

Should you place your hands together when saying いただきます？

In the left 4-panel comic, Tanaka-san and Egg-san are placing their hands together while saying いただきます. While it's not rude to say いただきます without the gesture, doing so creates a more polite impression. It's also worth noting that in Japan it's less common to see this kind of gesture when saying ありがとうございます.

In some countries, there's a cultural tradition of placing your hands together like this to express gratitude, but in Japan it's more common to bow slightly instead.

お水 おねがいします。

Omizu onegai shimasu.

Could I get some water?

Omizu onegai shimasu.
Could I get some water?

Doozo.
Here you are.

A, sumimasen...
Oh, my bad...

Kore, raamen no suupu deshita.
That's ramen soup.

This is a phrase used to ask for a refill of water at a restaurant. Other countries may not provide free water but in Japan not only is water free but some restaurants even provide complimentary tea, such as barley tea. It's also common for water to have ice in it, even during winter. Along with water, you may also experience a complimentary hand towel called おしぼり (oshibori) to wipe your hands before your meal.

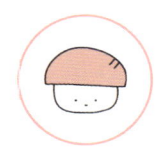

すみません、
フォーク おねがいします。
Sumimasen, fooku onegai shimasu.
Excuse me, could I get a fork?

◁)) 18-2

かしこまりました。どうぞ。
Kashikomarimashita. Doozo.
You got it. Here you are.

Phrase Practice

Let's try saying the below sentence
with the following words inside the parentheses.

◁)) 18-3

(　　　) おねがいします。
(　　　) onegai shimasu.
Could I get a (　　)?

おさら
osara
plate

スプーン
supuun
spoon

おはし
ohashi
pair of chopsticks

\ Tips /
from Tanaka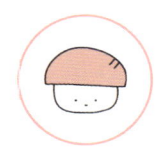

Let's get an おかわり (okawari)

A refill is referred to as おかわり in Japanese. So, when you want a refill of water, you can phrase it like this:

お水 おかわり おねがいします。
Omizu okawari onegai shimasu.
Could I get a refill of water?

Similarly, if you want to order another beer, you can say:

ビール おかわり おねがいします。
Biiru okawari onegai shimasu.
Could I get another beer?

Additionally, at some restaurants, you may have the option of a rice refill with your meal (sometimes free-of-charge, sometimes at an additional cost). In such cases, you can say:

ごはん おかわり おねがいします。
Gohan okawari onegai shimasu.
Could I get another serving of rice?

おかいけい おねがいします。

Okaikee onegai shimasu.
Could we get the check?

Okaikee onegai shimasu.
Could we get the check?

Tanaka san, koko wa watashi ga haraimasu.
Tanaka-san, it's on me.

Ieie, watashi ga haraimasu.
No, no, it's on me.

Jaa onegai shimasu.
Oh, well if you insist.

This is a phrase used when you finish your meal and want to ask for the check. When you call out to the staff with this, they should bring it to you. In restaurants with a cashier at the entrance, you take the check to the register to pay. However, in places like ramen shops or standing soba noodle restaurants — where you buy your meal ticket upfront — you can simply say ごちそうさまでした (Gochisoosama deshita → Phrase 20) and leave without needing to ask for the check.

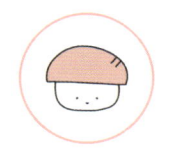

すみません、
おかいけい おねがいします。
Sumimasen, okaikee onegai shimasu.
Excuse me. Could I get the check?

Conversation Example ◁)) 19-2

はい、しょうしょう おまちください。
Hai, shooshoo omachi kudasai.
You got it. Give me a moment.

Vocabulary related to the bill

Vocabulary ◁)) 19-3

でんぴょう
dempyoo
voucher

レシート
reshiito
receipt

おつり
otsuri
change

\ Tips / from Tanaka

The no tipping culture of Japan

In Japan, there is no established tipping culture. Even if you try to leave a tip, in most cases, it will not be accepted. Even saying "Keep the change" when you receive your change can actually inconvenience the staff. Simply paying the amount written on the bill should be fine.

ごちそうさまでした。

Gochisoosama deshita.
Thank you for the meal. (after eating)

🔊 20-1

Reshiito de gozaimasu.
Here is your receipt.

Gochisoosama deshita!
Thank you for the meal.

Mata kimasu.
We'll come again.

Jaa yoru mo doo desu ka?
How about tonight?

いただきます (Phrase 17) is indeed used before a meal, and so ごちそうさまでした is used after. It's a common phrase to express gratitude towards the food or the person who prepared it. It's a standard phrase to say aloud to the staff after finishing your meal and paying the check, so be sure to use it.

200円の おつりと
レシートで ございます。
にひゃく えん

Nihyaku en no otsuri to
reshiito de gozaimasu.
Here is your change of 200 yen and the receipt.

🔊 20-2

ごちそうさまでした。
Gochisoosama deshita.
Thank you for the meal.

ありがとうございました。
また おこしくださいませ。
Arigatoo gozaimashita.
Mata okoshi kudasai mase.
Thank you very much. Please come again.

\ Tips / from Tanaka

Japanese dining manners

In Japan, there are a variety of dining manners that differ from those in other countries.

First, *miso* soup and rice bowls are held in the hand and eaten directly from. However, you should not lift up communal or large plates that contain side dishes. When using chopsticks, it's considered taboo to skewer food with them or to pass food directly from your chopsticks to someone else's.

Additionally, making noise while chewing food is considered bad manners, although there are exceptions such as with soba or ramen, where slurping is acceptable.

PHRASE 21

おいしかったです。

Oishikatta desu.

The food was so good.

🔊 21-1

Ryoori wa doo deshita ka?
How was the food?

Oishikatta desu!
The food was so good!

Soo desu ka, yokatta desu.
I'm glad to hear it.

Nakanaide kudasai!
Please don't cry!

This is a phrase to express one's thoughts on the meal. If you're satisfied with the food, try saying this phrase in addition to ごちそうさまでした introduced on the previous page when paying the bill. It's a simple phrase, but I think it's the words that restaurant staff would most like to hear from customers.

こちら、レシートで ございます。
Kochira, reshiito de gozaimasu.
Here is your receipt.

Conversation Example 🔊 21-2

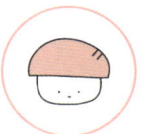

ごちそうさまでした。おいしかったです。
Gochisoosama deshita. Oishikatta desu.
Thank you for the meal. The food was so good.

よかったです。ありがとうございます。
Yokatta desu. Arigatoo gozaimasu.
Glad to hear it. Thank you so much.

Phrases to use before, during and after eating

Bonus Phrases 🔊 21-3

おいしそうです。	おいしいです。	おいしかったです。
Oishisoo desu.	Oishii desu.	Oishikatta desu.
It looks so good.	*It's so good.*	*It was so good.*
(before eating)	*(during eating)*	*(after eating)*

\ Tips / from Tanaka

Servers don't come by during meals

In restaurants overseas, it's common for a server to be assigned to each table and to come by during the meal to ask, "How is everything?" However, in Japan, it's not as common for the staff to approach tables during the meal to inquire about the food. If you want to express that the meal was enjoyable, it's best to do so at the end of the meal when paying the check.

How to Say "Dates" and "Day of the Week"

Month

1 月 ichi gatsu January	2 月 ni gatsu February	3 月 san gatsu March	4 月 shi gatsu April	5 月 go gatsu May	6 月 roku gatsu June
7 月 shichi gatsu July	8 月 hachi gatsu August	9 月 ku gatsu September	10 月 juu gatsu October	11 月 juuichi gatsu November	12 月 juuni gatsu December

Day

1 ついたち tsuitachi	2 ふつか futsuka	3 みっか mikka	4 よっか yokka	5 いつか itsuka	6 むいか muika	7 なのか nanoka
8 ようか yooka	9 ここのか kokonoka	10 とおか tooka	11 じゅういちにち juuichinichi	12 じゅうににち juuninichi	13 じゅうさんにち juusannichi	14 じゅうよっか juuyokka
15 じゅうごにち juugonichi	16 じゅうろくにち juurokunichi	17 じゅうしちにち juushichinichi	18 じゅうはちにち juuhachinichi	19 じゅうくにち juukunichi	20 はつか hatsuka	21 にじゅういちにち nijuuichinichi
22 にじゅうににち nijuuninichi	23 にじゅうさんにち nijuusannichi	24 にじゅうよっか nijuuyokka	25 にじゅうごにち nijuugonichi	26 にじゅうろくにち nijuurokunichi	27 にじゅうしちにち nijuushichinichi	28 にじゅうはちにち nijuuhachinichi
29 にじゅうくにち nijuukunichi	30 さんじゅうにち sanjuunichi	31 さんじゅういちにち sanjuuichinichi				

Day of the Week

月曜日 getsu yoobi Monday	火曜日 ka yoobi Tuesday	水曜日 sui yoobi Wednesday	木曜日 moku yoobi Thursday	金曜日 kin yoobi Friday
土曜日 do yoobi Saturday	日曜日 nichi yoobi Sunday			

Chapter

3

Shopping
Phrases

これは ありますか？

Kore wa arimasu ka?

Do you have this?

1

あの、すみません

Ano, sumimasen.
Um, excuse me.

2

これは ありますか？

Kore wa arimasu ka?
Do you have this?

3

はい、こちらに ありますよ

Hai, kochira ni arimasu yo.
Yes, just over here.

4

そのかしゅは わたしのいもうとです

Sono kashu wa watashi no imooto desu.
The singer is my sister.

This is a phrase used to inquire about whether a store has what you are looking for. In stores like 100-yen shops or drugstores, there are often many items, making it difficult to find what you're looking for. Additionally, you might not know the name of the item you want in Japanese. You can use this phrase while pulling up a photo on your smartphone to show the store clerk as you ask.

すみません、これは ありますか？
Sumimasen, kore wa arimasu ka?
Excuse me, do you have this?

🔊 22-2

もうしわけございません。
それは ありません。
Mooshiwake gozaimasen. Sore wa arimasen.
I'm sorry, but we don't have it.

Phrase Practice

Let's try saying the below sentence
with the following words inside the parentheses.

🔊 22-3

（　　　）は ありますか？
（　　　）wa arimasu ka?
Do you have (　　)?

この キャラクターの
グッズ
kono kyarakutaa no guzzu
this character merchandise

英語の
メニュー
（えいご）
eego no menyuu
an English menu

\ Tips /
from Tanaka

Returning or exchanging an item

When you accidentally purchase the wrong item or if there is a defect in the product, you can use the following phrases to inquire about returning or exchanging it:

へんぴん できますか？
Hempin dekimasu ka?
Can I return this?

こうかん できますか？
Kookan dekimasu ka?
Can I exchange this?

In many cases, you will need the receipt from when you bought it. The policies regarding returns and exchanges often vary depending on the store. It's advisable to check with the staff for confirmation.

大きい サイズは ありますか？
<ruby>大<rt>おお</rt></ruby>

Ookii saizu wa arimasu ka?

Do you have this in a larger size?

Sukoshi chiisai desu ne.
It's a bit small.

Ookii saizu wa arimasu ka?
Do you have this in a larger size?

Sore ga ichiban ookii saizu desu.
That is the largest we have.
Ato sukoshi...!
If you just keep...

A!
Ah!

This is a phrase you can use when out buying clothes or shoes. Since sizing standards may differ between Japan and other countries, it's best to try on the item before purchasing rather than relying solely on what the size on the tag says. When using the fitting room, it's polite to check with the staff first by asking, しちゃくしても いいですか？ (Shichaku shite mo ii desu ka?, *Can I try this on?*) before doing so.

いかがですか？
Ikaga desu ka?
What do you think?

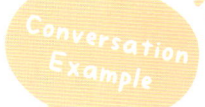

🔊 23-2

うーん…。ちがう 色は ありますか？
Uuun... Chigau iro wa arimasu ka?
Mmm... Do you have this in a different color?

はい、おまちください。
Hai, omachi kudasai.
Yes we do. Just one moment.

Phrase Practice

Let's try saying the below sentence with the following words inside the parentheses.

🔊 23-3

（　　　）は ありますか？
（　　　）wa arimasu ka?
Do you have this in a (　　　)?

小さい サイズ	ちがう 色	ちがう デザイン
chiisai saizu	chigau iro	chigau dezain
smaller size	*different color*	*different design*

\ Tips / from Tanaka

Responding to いらっしゃいませ (Irasshaimase)

When entering a clothing store or similar establishment, you may hear the staff greet you with いらっしゃいませ. While it's perfectly fine to respond with こんにちは or any other greeting, simply nodding or acknowledging with a slight bow is also acceptable. Moreover, if a staff member approaches you while you're browsing and asks, "Need help finding anything?," and you don't intend to make a purchase, you can politely respond with:

見ているだけです。ありがとうございます。
Miteiru dake desu. Arigatoo gozaimasu.
I'm just looking, thank you.

これに します。

Kore ni shimasu.

I'll go with this.

Kore ni shimasu.
I'll go with this.

A... Yappari kore ni shimasu.
Hm... Actually, I'll go with this one instead.

Yappari moo sukoshi mimasu.
Actually, I'm going to look around some more.

This is a phrase used to indicate one's intention to purchase something while shopping. It's used not only in clothing stores but also when ordering at restaurants. As mentioned in Phrase 14, if the item is near the listener, you can say それに します (Sore ni shimasu, *I'll go with that*), and if it's far from both you and the listener, you can say あれに します (Are ni shimasu, *I'll go with that one over there*).

この ネックレスは
とても おすすめです。
Kono nekkuresu wa totemo osusume desu.
I highly recommend this necklace.

🔊 24-2

Conversation Example

じゃあ、これに します。
Jaa, kore ni shimasu.
Okay, I'll go with this.

\ Tips / from Tanaka

これ ください (*This please*) & これに します (*I'll go with this*)

If you have studied Japanese before, you may have learned that これ ください (Kore kudasai) translates to "I'll take this." While it is true that これ ください is also a commonly used expression, it seems a bit direct. On the other hand, これに します has a nuance of "I've considered several products and decided on this one." Like Tofu-san in the 4-panel comic strip, これに します is more appropriate when you have decided what to buy after a lot of deliberation.

ホットコーヒーを 1つ
おねがいします。

Hotto koohii o hitotsu onegai shimasu.
I'll have a hot coffee, please.

Irasshaimase.
Welcome to our business.

Hotto koohii o hitotsu
onegai shimasu.
I'll have a hot coffee, please.

'Ka... Kawaii...!'
'Sh-she's so cute!'

Ano...
Hotto koohii onegai shimasu...
Um... My hot coffee, please...

This is a phrase used when placing an order. "What" and "how many" you want to order are the most important pieces of information the staff needs. Especially 1つ (hitotsu, *one*) and 2つ (futatsu, *two*) sound similar in pronunciation and can be easily misunderstood, so clear pronunciation is key. It's also helpful to use hand gestures to indicate the number to ensure your order is understood accurately.

いらっしゃいませ。
Irasshaimase.
Welcome to our business.

🔊 25-2

アイスコーヒーを １つと
サンドイッチを ２つ おねがいします。
Aisu koohii o hitotsu to sandoicchi o futatsu
onegai shimasu.
I'll have one iced coffee and two sandwiches, please.

かしこまりました。
おかいけい 1,500円でございます。
Kashikomarimashita.
Okaikee sengohyaku en de gozaimasu.
Very well. Your total will be 1,500 yen.

Counting numbers

🔊 25-3

１つ
hitotsu
one

２つ
futatsu
two

３つ
mittsu
three

４つ
yottsu
four

５つ
itsutsu
five

６つ
muttsu
six

７つ
nanatsu
seven

８つ
yattsu
eight

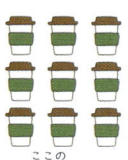
９つ
kokonotsu
nine

67

PHRASE 26

いくらですか？
Ikura desu ka?
How much?

🔊 26-1

Kore wa ikura desu ka?
How much is this?

Sambyaku en desu.
300 yen.

Yasui desu ne!
That's so cheap!

Jaa, samman en desu.
Ah, then 30,000 yen.

This is a phrase used to ask about the price of an item. When shopping or dining out, sometimes prices may not be listed. To avoid surprises at the register when paying, it's helpful to use this phrase to confirm the price beforehand so you can fully enjoy your shopping or dining experience.

これは いくらですか？
Kore wa ikura desu ka?
How much is this?

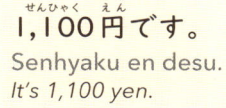

1,100円です。
せんひゃく　えん
Senhyaku en desu.
It's 1,100 yen.

じゃあ、これに します。
Jaa, kore ni shimasu.
Okay, I'll go with this one.

Bonus Phrases

◁» 26-3

Price phrases

やすいですね。
Yasui desu ne.
That's so cheap.

たかいですね。
Takai desu ne.
That's so expensive.

\ Tips / from Tanaka

Japan consumption tax

Consumption tax is a tax imposed on the sale of goods and the provision of services. As of 2024 the current tax is 10% which is applied to most goods (though some items, such as food products, including takeout, are taxed at 8%).

Foreign tourists may be eligible for tax-free shopping on items purchased at tax-free shops such as department stores and electronics retailers. If you shop at a store labeled as "Tax Free," you can ask about how to use it.

クレジットカードは つかえますか？

Kurejitto kaado wa tsukaemasu ka?

Do you accept credit cards?

🔊 27-1

Kurejitto kaado wa tsukaemasu ka?
Do you accept credit cards?

Hai, tsukaemasu yo!
Yes, we do!

... Kore, kurejitto kaado ja nai desu.
...This is not a credit card.

Aaa! Machigaemashita!
Ahhh! I gave the wrong one!

This phrase can be used to ask about the availability of your preferred payment method when you go to pay. Many convenience stores and chain stores in Japan accept lots of different payment methods such as credit cards, mobile payments, and electronic money. However, smaller shops and street stalls often only accept cash, so it's a good idea to keep some cash on hand just in case.

クレジットカードは つかえますか？

Kurejitto kaado wa tsukaemasu ka?

Do you accept credit cards?

🔊 27-2

すみません、げんきんしか つかえません。

Sumimasen, genkin shika tsukaemasen.

I'm sorry, but we only accept cash.

Phrase Practice

Let's try saying the below sentence with the following words inside the parentheses.

🔊 27-3

（　　　）は つかえますか？

（　　　）wa tsukaemasu ka?

Could I use (　　)?

この カード
kono kaado
this card

この クーポン
kono kuupon
this coupon

Tips from Tanaka

Types of coins and bills

Here you can learn about the different types of Japanese coins and bills. All of them feature intricate patterns and designs. For example, the 10 yen coin depicts the Byodoin Temple in Kyoto, while the 100 yen coin features cherry blossoms. If you have the opportunity to see some Japanese coins and bills, be sure to check out their designs.

Coins						
	1 yen	5 yen	10 yen	50 yen	100 yen	500 yen

Bills	1,000 yen	2,000 yen (rare)	5,000 yen	10,000 yen

Formal "Keigo" and Casual "Tameguchi"

All the phrases featured in this book are examples of formal speech, referred to as 敬語 (keigo). *Keigo* is used when speaking to people you have just met, those you are not very close to, or people like superiors or colleagues in the workplace. On the other hand, there is also casual speech, known as タメ口 (tameguchi), which is used to communicate with friends, family, and other close acquaintances.

敬語 Keigo (*formal*)	タメ口 Tameguchi (*casual*)
おはようございます。 Ohayoo gozaimasu. *Good morning.*	おはよう。 Ohayoo. *Morning.*
おやすみなさい。 Oyasumi nasai. *Good night.*	おやすみ。 Oyasumi. *Night.*
ありがとうございます。 Arigatoo gozaimasu. *Thank you.*	ありがとう。 Arigatoo. *Thanks.*
はい。／いいえ。 Hai. / Iie. *Yes. / No.*	うん。／ううん。 Un. / Uun. *Yup. / Nope.*
おつかれさまです。 Otsukaresama desu. *Great work today.*	おつかれさま。 Otsukaresama. *Nice work.*

Chapter

4

Sightseeing Phrases

PHRASE 28

チェックイン　おねがいします。

Chekku in onegai shimasu.
I'd like to check in.

🔊 28-1

Chekku in onegai shimasu.
I'd like to check in.

Eggu sama desu ne.
Alright, Mr. Egg.

'Pasupooto no shashin...'
'This passport photo...'

Aa, sannem mae no shashin desu.
Oh, that photo is from 3 years ago.

You use this phrase when you first arrive at a hotel or *ryokan*. Afterwards, you may be asked for your name, reservation number, or to present your passport, so simply answer any of the questions you're asked. When checking out, you just say チェックアウト　おねがいします (Chekku auto onegai shimasu).

チェックイン おねがいします。
Chekku in onegai shimasu.
I'd like to check in.

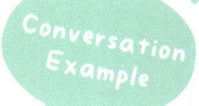
Conversation Example
🔊 28-2

おなまえを おねがいします。
Onamae o onegai shimasu.
May I have your name?

エッグです。
Eggu desu.
It's Egg.

Phrases for use in accommodations

Bonus Phrases
🔊 28-3

よやく
しています。
Yoyaku
shite imasu.
*I made a
reservation.*

ルームサービス
おねがいします。
Ruumu saabisu
onegai shimasu.
*Room service
please.*

にもつを
あずけたいです。
Nimotsu o
azuketai desu.
*I'd like to leave
my luggage.*

\ Tips / from Tanaka

Types of accommodations

There's a variety of accommodation options beyond the typical Western-style hotels.

For instance, a *ryokan* is a Japanese-style inn where you can stay in *tatami*-mat rooms, relish traditional Japanese cuisine, and unwind in hot springs. In a *ryokan*, it's customary to remove your shoes at the entrance, like in a typical Japanese home, so remember not to step inside with your shoes on.

Another type are "capsule hotels," featuring small capsule-like sleeping units with shared facilities such as toilets and showers. Their compact size aside, capsule hotels offer more privacy compared to dormitory-style hostels, making them ideal for solo travelers or those seeking to cut down on accommodation expenses.

Wi-Fiは ありますか？

Waifai wa arimasu ka?

Is there Wi-Fi available?

すみません、
Wi-Fiはありますか？

Sumimasen, waifai wa arimasu ka?
Excuse me, is there Wi-Fi available?

はい、こちらです

Hai, kochira desu.
Yes, here you are.

わたしの電話番号です

070 - xxxx - xxxx

デート
してください

Watashi no denwa bangoo desu:
"deeto shite kudasai."
My Phone Number:
"Please go out with me."

はやくWi-Fiを
おしえてください

Hayaku waifai o oshiete kudasai.
Could you just tell me the Wi-Fi
information?

This phrase is used to ask about the availability of Wi-Fi at accommodations, cafes, or other places. When traveling, access to the internet is essential for looking up information about places to visit and navigating your way. While some may opt to purchase a SIM card for their stay in Japan, many visitors with shorter stays rely on free Wi-Fi networks as their primary means of connectivity. In recent years, the number of spots offering free Wi-Fi has increased, so it's worth learning how to use this phrase.

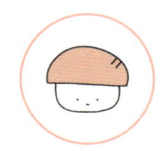

Wi-Fiは ありますか？
Waifai wa arimasu ka?
Is there Wi-Fi available?

🔊 29-2

すみません、ここは Wi-Fiが ありません。
Sumimasen, koko wa waifai ga arimasen.
I'm sorry, but we don't.

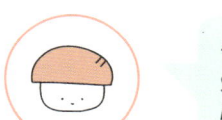

そうですか。わかりました。
Soo desu ka. Wakarimashita.
I see. Thanks.

Bonus Phrase

🔊 29-3

Ask for Wi-Fi password

Wi-Fiの パスワードは なんですか？
Waifai no pasuwaado wa nan desu ka?
What is the Wi-Fi password?

\ Tips / from Tanaka

About free Wi-Fi

In Japan, there used to be fewer spots with Wi-Fi access compared to a lot of places overseas. However, in recent years, with the boom in tourism, the number of free Wi-Fi spots has increased a lot, and you can now find them in various places such as:

- Shinkansen (bullet trains)
- Train stations
- Shopping malls
- Tourist attractions
- Cafes

PHRASE 30

東京駅に 行きたいのですが。

とうきょうえき／い

Tookyoo eki ni ikitai no desu ga.

How do I get to Tokyo Station?

🔊 30-1

Kyoo wa Ichigo chan no raibu.
Today is Ichigo-chan's concert.

Sumimasen,
Tookyoo eki ni ikitai no desu ga.
Excuse me,
how do I get to Tokyo Station?

Sam bansen no densha ni
notte kudasai.
You can take the train on track No.3.

'Minna Ichigo chan no fan...?!'
'They're all Ichigo-chan fans...?!'

This phrase is used when you want to ask for directions to your destination. In cities like Tokyo or Osaka, there are lots of train and bus routes, and transfers can get complicated. On top of that, station names can be long and difficult to remember. To get to your destination smoothly, use this phrase to ask someone nearby for directions.

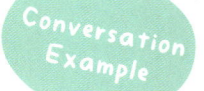

すみません、秋葉原に 行きたいのですが。
Sumimasen, Akihabara ni ikitai no desu ga.
Excuse me, how do I get to Akihabara?

🔊 30-2

ちかてつに のってください。
Chikatetsu ni notte kudasai.
You can take the subway.

わかりました。ありがとうございます。
Wakarimashita. Arigatoo gozaimasu.
I see. Thank you so much.

Phrase Practice

Let's try saying the below sentence
with the following words inside the parentheses.

(　　　)に 行きたいのですが。
(　　　)ni ikitai no desu ga.
How do I get to (　　　)?

🔊 30-3

成田空港
Narita kuukoo
Narita Airport

浅草
Asakusa

ここ
koko
this place here
(pointing at a map)

\ Tips /
from Tanaka

Manners with public transportation

In Japan, there are several manners and etiquettes to keep in mind when using public transportation like trains and buses. While not following these guidelines won't get you in any serious trouble, it's a good idea to be aware of them; otherwise you might end up with some dirty looks from fellow passengers:

– Line up before boarding.
– Avoid speaking loudly.
– Refrain from talking on the phone.
– Do not eat or drink (although it's generally acceptable on long-distance trains like the shinkansen).
– Give priority seats to elderly or physically impaired individuals.

しゃしんを とりましょうか？

Shashin o torimashoo ka?
Would you like me to take a picture?

Shashin o torimashoo ka?
Would you like me to take a picture?

Yokattara issho ni torimashoo!
We can take one all together if you like!

Jaa, watashi ga torimashoo ka?
How about I take the picture?

You can use this phrase to offer to take a photo for someone who seems like they want to take one. Lots of people take selfies at tourist spots, but if you see someone who seems to be having trouble taking a photo, try asking them this. And when you want someone to take a photo of you, it's easier to ask after taking their photo first.

しゃしんを とりましょうか？
Shashin o torimashoo ka?
Would you like me to take a picture?

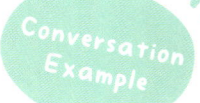

🔊 31-2

おねがいします。
Onegai shimasu.
Yes, please.

はい、チーズ！
Hai, chiizu!
Say cheese!

ありがとうございます。
Arigatoo gozaimasu.
Thank you so much.

🔊 31-3

Ask for taking a photo together

いっしょに しゃしんを とりませんか？
Issho ni shashin o torimasen ka?
Would you like to take a picture together?

\ Tips / from Tanaka

Calls for pictures

In photography, there is a classic phrase used by the person shooting:

はい、チーズ！ (Hai, chiizu!)

This expression is a direct translation of the English phrase "Say cheese!" However, unlike in English, the person being photographed does not say "Cheese!" Instead, it serves as a signal indicating "I'm about to take the picture."

しゃしんを とってもらえますか？

Shashin o totte moraemasu ka?

Can you take a picture for me?

1

すみません、
しゃしんをとって
もらえますか？

Sumimasen,
shashin o totte moraemasu ka?
Excuse me. Can you take a picture for us?

2

はい、
もちろんです！

Hai, mochiron desu!
Sure, of course!

3

とりますよ〜

Torimasu yo.
Here we go...!

4

はい、チーズ！

Hai, chiizu!
Say cheese!

This is a phrase that can be used when you want someone else to take a photo of you, in contrast to the previous phrase. While you can use a selfie stick or other devices to take photos by yourselves, asking someone else to take the photo might create a good opportunity for interaction and make for a memorable experience. It's often smooth to ask someone who is standing right behind you or someone you've just taken a photo for.

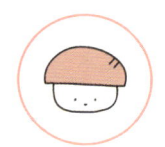

すみません、しゃしんを
とってもらえますか？

Sumimasen, shashin o totte
moraemasu ka?
Excuse me, can you take a picture for me?

Conversation Example

🔊 32-2

はい、いいですよ。

Hai, ii desu yo.
Yeah, of course.

ありがとうございます。

Arigatoo gozaimasu.
Thank you so much.

\ Tips / from Tanaka

Posing for a photo

In Japan, it's very common for people to make the peace sign when taking photos, as shown in the illustration below. It's a classic pose for photos, and it doesn't necessarily have a deep meaning. Many people just reflexively make a peace sign when a camera is pointed at them.

People may use both hands or make the sign near their face, and varies from person to person. When you visit tourist spots, it can be fun to observe the different poses Japanese people use when taking photos.

この おかしは どこで 買えますか?

Kono okashi wa doko de kaemasu ka?

Where can I get this treat?

Kono okashi wa doko de kaemasu ka?
Where can I get this treat?

Koko de kaemasu yo!
You can get it right here!

Shooshoo omachi kudasai.
Give me a moment.

Gohyaku en desu.
That'll be 500 yen.

This is a phrase used to ask where something can be obtained. It can be used for different purposes, such as when you want to buy local specialties, train tickets, or medication. When you don't know the name of the product or find it difficult to explain it in words, showing a photo on your smartphone while asking the store clerk can make it easier to communicate what you're looking for.

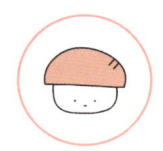

この ぬいぐるみは どこで 買えますか？
Kono nuigurumi wa doko de kaemasu ka?
Where can I get this stuffed animal?

ここで 買えます。
Koko de kaemasu.
You can buy it here.

Let's try saying the below sentence
with the following words inside the parentheses.

(　　　) は どこで 買えますか？
(　　　) wa doko de kaemasu ka?
Where can I get (　　)?

| チケット
chiketto
a ticket | 電車の
フリーパス
densha no furiipasu
unlimited ride pass | 水
mizu
some water |

\ Tips / from Tanaka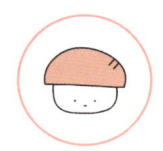

Recommended Japanese souvenirs

Here are some recommendations for souvenirs if you want to bring them back for family, friends or yourself.

Snacks that are easy to split are a good option. Japanese specialty flavors like *matcha* are especially popular. Traditional Japanese crafts are also a good choice. For those concerned about breakage, small and lightweight items like chopsticks and chopstick rests are ideal.

Additionally, 100-yen shops offer interesting and practical items at low prices, making them perfect for finding plenty of affordable souvenirs.

Bringing back Japanese books or manga as souvenirs is also a great idea. Browsing various books at bookstores can be enjoyable, and it can serve as motivation for Japanese language learning even after returning home. I hope you find some great souvenirs!

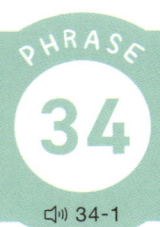
この　バスは　清水寺に
行きますか？

Kono basu wa Kiyomizudera ni ikimasu ka?

Does this bus go to Kiyomizu-dera Temple?

Sumimasen.
Excuse me.

Kono basu wa Kiyomizudera ni ikimasu ka?
Does this bus go to Kiyomizu-dera Temple?

Iie, ikimasen.
No, it doesn't.
Ano basu ni notte kudasai.
You should take that one over there.

A... Are desu ka...?
T-that one...?

You can use this phrase when you want to confirm if the bus you are about to board goes to your desired destination. In popular tourist destinations like Kyoto, buses are more well developed than trains. There are a large number of bus routes, so it's easy to accidentally get on the wrong bus and end up going far away from your intended destination. It's a good idea to confirm with the driver before boarding to ensure you have enough time for sightseeing.

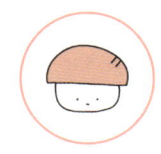

この 電車は 名古屋駅に 行きますか？

Kono densha wa Nagoya eki ni ikimasu ka?

Does this train go to Nagoya Station?

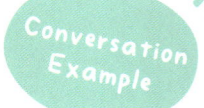

🔊 34-2

いいえ、行きません。
3ばんせんの 電車に のってください。

Iie, ikimasen. Sam bansen no densha ni notte kudasai.

No, it doesn't. You should take the train on track No.3.

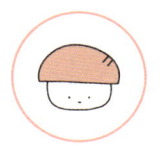

わかりました。ありがとうございます。

Wakarimashita. Arigatoo gozaimasu.

Understood. Thank you so much.

Phrase Practice

🔊 34-3

. . . .
Let's try saying the below sentence
with the following words inside the parentheses.
. . . .

この バスは （　　　）に 行きますか？

Kono basu wa (　　) ni ikimasu ka?

Does this bus go to (　　)?

京都駅	金閣寺	八坂神社
Kyooto eki	Kinkakuji	Yasaka jinja
Kyoto Station	*Kinkaku-ji Temple*	*Yasaka Shrine*

 \ Tips / from Tanaka

Enjoy visiting shrines and temples

There are shrines and temples all throughout Japan. While learning about the history and admiring their architecture and gardens is enjoyable in its own right, I'd like to introduce an item that can enhance your experience even more: おまもり (omamori).

Omamori are small, these pouch-like items that you can purchase at shrines and temples. It is believed that carrying these can protect you from evil spirits and bring you good fortune. There are *omamori* for different purposes like health, traffic safety, and academic success.

Since the designs of *omamori* vary depending on the shrine or temple, collecting *omamori* from different places could also be an activity to enjoy.

なん時からですか？

Nan ji kara desu ka?

What time does it start?

🔊 35-1

Hanabi taikai wa nan ji kara desu ka?

What time does the fireworks festival start?

E? Hanabi taikai desu ka?

Fireworks festival?

Moo owarimashita yo?

It's been over.

Joodan desu, hachi ji kara desu.

Kidding. It starts at 8 PM.

This phrase is used to ask about an event's starting time or when a shop opens. Japan's culture places an importance on punctuality, so events typically start promptly at the scheduled time. Additionally, when asking about the closing time of an event or the closing hours of a shop, you can use the phrase なん時までですか？ (Nan ji made desu ka?).

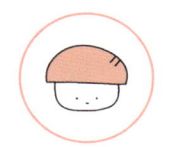

ライブは なん時からですか？

Raibu wa nan ji kara desu ka?

What time does the concert start?

🔊 35-2

11時からです。

Juuichi ji kara desu.

It starts at 11.

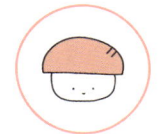

わかりました。
ありがとうございます。

Wakarimashita.
Arigatoo gozaimasu.

I see. Thank you so much.

Vocabulary

🔊 35-3

How to say time

1時
ichi ji
one o'clock

2時
ni ji
two o'clock

3時
san ji
three o'clock

4時
yo ji
four o'clock

5時
go ji
five o'clock

6時
roku ji
six o'clock

7時
shichi ji
seven o'clock

8時
hachi ji
eight o'clock

9時
ku ji
nine o'clock

10時
juu ji
ten o'clock

11時
juuichi ji
eleven o'clock

12時
juuni ji
twelve o'clock

36

トイレは どこですか？

Toire wa doko desu ka?

Where is the bathroom?

🔊 36-1

すみません…

Sumimasen...
Excuse me...

トイレは どこですか…？

Toire wa doko desu ka...?
Where is the bathroom...?

トイレは あそこです

どうしましたか？

Toire wa asoko desu.
It's right over there.
Doo shimashita ka?
Are you okay?

きのうケーキを 30こたべました

Kinoo keeki o sanjukko tabemashita.
I ate 30 pieces of cake yesterday.

You can use this phrase when asking about the location of something. Public toilets in some places overseas require coins to be inserted at the entrance, but in Japan, public toilets are mostly free to use and are often very clean.

 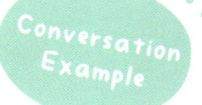
すみません、コンビニは どこですか？
Sumimasen, kombini wa doko desu ka?
Excuse me, where is a convenience store?

🔊 36-2

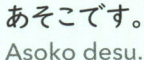 

あそこです。
Asoko desu.
Over there.

わかりました。ありがとうございます。
Wakarimashita. Arigatoo gozaimasu.
Understood. Thank you.

Phrase Practice

🔊 36-3

Let's try saying the below sentence with the following words inside the parentheses.

（　　　）は どこですか？
（　　　）wa doko desu ka?
Where is (　　　)?

駅 (えき)	りょうがえじょ	びょういん
eki	ryoogaejo	byooin
the station	*an exchange counter*	*the hospital*

＼Tips／ from Tanaka

All the buttons on the toilet

In toilets, you may find a lot of different functions. You might sometimes see English or other languages, but there are lots of times where there's only Japanese or illustrations, which can lead to confusion about which one to press.

You'll usually find the following buttons:

大 (だい) dai   *big flush*: flush with a large amount of water
小 (しょう) shoo   *small flush*: flush with a small amount of water
おしり oshiri   *washlet*: for cleaning the butt
ビデ bide   *bidet*
呼び出し (よ・だ) yobidashi   *call attendant/emergency*: to call for assistance in case of emergency or discomfort

Be careful not to mistake the emergency call button for the flush buttons.

Honorific Titles "San, Sama, Chan, Kun"

In Japanese, we have lots of honorific titles we use depending on the age, gender, and relationship with the person we're talking to or about. But here I'm just going to cover four of the most common.

san

This is a polite honorific that can be used regardless of gender. You use it when addressing someone you are meeting for the first time, it's good to use "(Surname) + san."
For example: 田中さん

sama

This honorific title is even more polite than "san." It's most commonly used by shop staff when they are addressing customers.
For example: 田中さま

chan

This is a really casual honorific mostly used with women. Though, it also gets used with young children, regardless of gender. It is an affectionate way of addressing someone and is not commonly used in formal settings like the workplace.
For example: とうふちゃん

kun

This honorific is mostly used with men. It's similar to "chan," as it is a casual title, but it is often used in the workplace when addressing male subordinates or colleagues.
For example: たこやきくん

You can also refer to others without using any honorific, like saying just "Tanaka" this is called *yobisute*. *Yobisute* is used with close friends, and it can be considered rude to use *yobisute* with people you are not very close to.

Chapter

5

More Conversational Phrases

PHRASE 37

あついですね。

Atsui desu ne.
Sure is hot today.

🔊 37-1

Atsui desu ne.
Sure is hot today.

Soo desu ne.
Yeah, it is.

Aisu doozo.
Have some ice cream.

You can use this phrase for small talk. Talking about the weather is a convenient topic that you can discuss with anyone. Especially in Japan, where changes in the four seasons can feel distinct, it's common to talk about the weather, temperature, and seasons. When you want to talk to someone but don't know what to talk about, why not try discussing the weather?

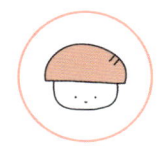

Conversation Example

🔊 37-2

ふじさん、こんにちは。
今日は あついですね。

Fuji san, konnichiwa.
Kyoo wa atsui desu ne.

Hi, Fuji-san. It's hot today, isn't it?

そうですね。むしあついですね。

Soo desu ne. Mushiatsui desu ne.

Yeah, it's hot and humid.

Weather phrases

Bonus Phrases

🔊 37-3

さむいですね。

Samui desu ne.

Sure is cold today.

あたたかいですね。

Atatakai desu ne.

Sure is nice and warm today.

いい 天気ですね。

Ii tenki desu ne.

It's so nice out today.

Tips from Tanaka

Four seasons in Japan

In Japanese, the four seasons are called the following:

はる	haru	*Spring*
なつ	natsu	*Summer*
あき	aki	*Autumn*
ふゆ	fuyu	*Winter*

Japan can feel like it has four distinct seasons, allowing people to enjoy the natural transitions such as cherry blossoms in spring and autumn foliage in autumn. Additionally, each season features various events and festivals, and it's characteristic for stores like convenience stores to sell seasonal limited-edition snacks. When you come to Japan, be sure to experience the pleasures of each season!

おつかれさまです。

Otsukaresama desu.
Otsukaresama desu.

Otsukaresama desu.
Otsukaresama desu.

Otsukaresama desu.
Otsukaresama desu.

Tadaima.
I'm home!

Toofu san, otsukaresama desu.
Tofu-san, otsukaresama desu.

There's no direct English equivalent for this phrase. It expresses appreciation and gratitude for someone's hard work or effort, and is often used among colleagues or members of the same community to acknowledge and thank each other. While primarily used in a workplace setting, it can also be used as a casual greeting or farewell outside of work when meeting or parting ways.

ぶちょう、おつかれさまです。
おさきに しつれいします。

Buchoo, otsukaresama desu.
Osaki ni shitsuree shimasu.
*Manager, otsukaresama desu. I'm
leaving for today, have a good evening.*

とうふさん、おつかれさま。

Toofu san, otsukaresama.
Otsukaresama, Tofu-san.

\ Tips /
from Tanaka

Isn't the parting greeting さようなら (Sayoonara)?

In the previous 4-panel comic strip, Tofu-san says おつかれさまです instead of さようなら when leaving work and going home. You might be wondering, "Isn't さようなら the usual way to say goodbye?" In reality, さようなら is not commonly used in everyday life. While it may be used in schools when greeting teachers or seniors, it's more formal and ceremonial, similar to "goodbye" or "farewell" in English, and is not often used casually. Instead, the following phrases are more commonly used as parting greetings:

おつかれさまです。
Otsukaresama desu.
Great work today.

しつれいします。
Shitsuree shimasu.
Pardon me.

Alternatively, among close acquaintances, you might hear:

じゃあね。
Jaa ne.
Later.

またね。
Mata ne.
Till next time.

バイバイ。
Baibai.
Bye bye.

だいじょうぶですか？
Daijoobu desu ka?
Are you okay?

Daijoobu desu ka?
Are you okay?

Hai, daijoobu desu.
Yes, I'm fine.

Ari no retsu o mite imasu.
I'm just watching this line of ants.

This is a phrase used to show concern for someone. だいじょうぶ translates to "fine" in English. If you notice someone looking unwell or in distress, it's kind to check on them by using this phrase.

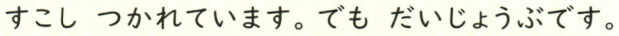

Conversation Example

だいじょうぶですか？
Daijoobu desu ka?
Are you okay?

39-2

すこし　つかれています。でも　だいじょうぶです。
Sukoshi tsukarete imasu. Demo daijoobu desu.
I'm just a little bit tired, but I'm fine.

おだいじに　してください。
Odaiji ni shite kudasai.
Please take care of yourself.

Bonus Phrases

39-3

Phrases of states

元気です。
Genki desu.
I'm doing well.

つかれています。
Tsukarete imasu.
I'm tired.

おなかが　すいています。
Onaka ga suite imasu.
I'm hungry.

\ Tips / from Tanaka

Phrases that show concern for the other person

If someone you know tells you they aren't feeling well, have caught a cold, or have been hospitalized, it's considerate to respond with the following phrases:

ゆっくり　やすんでください。 Yukkuri yasunde kudasai.
Please take it easy.

おだいじに　してください。 Odaiji ni shite kudasai.
Take care and get well soon.

40

たのしいです。

Tanoshii desu.
This is fun.

🔊 40-1

Saa, yatte mimashoo.
Let's try now.

Joozu desu ne.
You're doing great.

Tanoshii desu!
This is fun!

Ano hito wa... puro desu ka?
Is that person... a pro?

You can use this phrase to express emotions. たのしい means feeling excited or delighted by doing something enjoyable or fun. When you experience something joyful or exciting, try expressing those feelings in words. It might even uplift the mood of those around you as well.

日本(にほん)での せいかつは
どうですか？

Nihon deno seekatsu wa doo desu ka?
How is life in Japan?

🔊 40-2

とても たのしいです。

Totemo tanoshii desu.
It's very fun.

Phrases to express various feelings

🔊 40-3

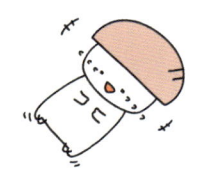

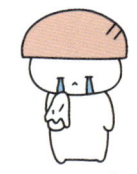

うれしいです。	おもしろいです。	かなしいです。
Ureshii desu.	Omoshiroi desu.	Kanashii desu.
I'm happy.	*I'm enjoying this.*	*I'm sad.*

Tips from Tanaka

Communicate how you felt in the past

By using the past tense of the above phrase,
you can express how you felt about past events.

たのしいです。　→　たのしかったです。
Tanoshii desu. 　Tanoshikatta desu.
This is fun. 　*It was fun.*

うれしいです。　→　うれしかったです。
Ureshii desu. 　Ureshikatta desu.
It makes me happy. 　*It made me happy.*

For example:

A:「きのうの のみかいは
　　どうでしたか？」

おもしろいです。→　おもしろかったです。
Omoshiroi desu. 　Omoshirokatta desu.
I'm enjoying this. 　*I enjoyed it.*

"Kinoo no nomikai wa doo deshita ka?"
"How was the party yesterday?"

かなしいです。　→　かなしかったです。
Kanashii desu. 　Kanashikatta desu.
I'm sad. 　*I was sad.*

B:「たのしかったです。」
"Tanoshikatta desu."
"It was fun."

きれい!

Kiree!
So pretty!

🔊 41-1

Waa...!
Wow...!

Kiree...!
So pretty...!

'Kiree...!'
'So pretty...!'

This phrase can be used as a soliloquy, to express your thoughts or feelings. The word きれい can be used to describe beautiful things like fireworks or even people. On the next page, many phrases that can be used as soliloquies are introduced. Try to practice these repeatedly so that when you experience something moving, the words come out without thinking.

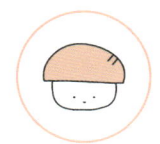

あれが　東京(とうきょう)スカイツリーです。
Are ga Tookyoo sukaitsurii desu.
That's the Tokyo Skytree.

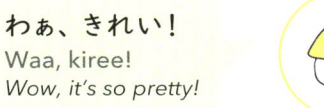

🔊 41-2

わぁ、きれい！
Waa, kiree!
Wow, it's so pretty!

Various soliloquy phrases

Bonus Phrases

🔊 41-3

かわいい！	かっこいい！	すてき！
Kawaii!	Kakkoii!	Suteki!
How cute!	*How cool!*	*How nice!*

おしゃれ！	すごい！	おもしろい！	びっくりした！
Oshare!	Sugoi!	Omoshiroi!	Bikkurishita!
How stylish!	*Amazing!*	*How funny!*	*How surprising!*

\ Tips /
from Tanaka

Japanese festivals

In Japan, there are lots of festivals with different characteristics in all the regions. Festivals have been held since ancient times to express gratitude and prayers to the gods. Many festivals are held in the summer, and some people wear *yukata* (a casual light summer *kimono*). People enjoy eating *takoyaki*, *yakisoba*, snow cones, and watching fireworks while going through all the food stalls.

Among the numerous festivals throughout Japan, the Gion Festival in Kyoto, the Tenjin Festival in Osaka, and the Kanda Festival in Tokyo are known as the "Three Great Festivals of Japan" and are particularly famous and large in scale. If you have the opportunity, try to attend one of them.

めん かRしRHで おねがいしRす。

Men katame de onegai shimasu.
Make the noodles firm please.

🔊 42-1

Tonkotsu raamen men katame de onegai shimasu.
Pork broth ramen and make the noodles firm, please.

Shooyu raamen men katame de onegai shimasu.
Shoyu ramen and make the noodles firm, please.

Omatase shimashita!
Here you go!

'Oishii...!'
'This is so good...!'

This is a phrase you can use at a ramen shop. If you're feeling confident with basic orders and want to step up your game a bit, give this phrase a try! In many ramen shops, you can specify the firmness of the noodles you prefer. If you like your noodles firm, you can use this phrase to request them, and they will adjust the cooking time accordingly to provide you with firmer noodles. And if you prefer softer noodles, you can say, めん やわらかめで おねがいします (Men yawarakame de onegai shimasu) to ask for softer noodles.

しょうゆ ラーメン 1つ、めん
やわらかめで おねがいします。

Shooyu raamen hitotsu, men
yawarakame de onegai shimasu.
*Shoyu ramen, and make the noodles
soft, please.*

🔊 42-2

Conversation
Example

かしこまりました。
Kashikomarimashita.
Very well.

Other phrases that can be used at ramen shops

Bonus
Phrases

🔊 42-3

おおもり おねがいします。	あじたま トッピング おねがいします。	かえだま おねがいします。
Oomori onegai shimasu. *Can I get that large size?*	Ajitama toppingu onegai shimasu. *Can I get a seasoned egg as a topping?*	Kaedama onegai shimasu. *Can I get a refill of noodles?*

\ Tips / from Tanaka

What to say when you want something left off

If you want to ask for something to be left off your order, you can use this phrase.

○○ ぬきで おねがいします。 ○○ nuki de onegai shimasu.
Please leave off the (something).

For example:

わさび ぬきで おねがいします。
Wasabi nuki de onegai shimasu.
Please leave off the wasabi.

たまねぎ ぬきで おねがいします。
Tamanegi nuki de onegai shimasu.
Please leave off the onion.

PHRASE 43

SNS やっていますか？

エスエヌエス

Esu-enu-esu yatte imasu ka?

Are you on any social media?

🔊 43-1

Toofu san.
Hey, Tofu-san.

Esu-enu-esu yatte imasu ka?
Are you on any social media?

Hai, kore ga watashi no akaunto desu.
Yeah, here's my account.

Forowaa hyakuman nin?!
You have a million followers?!

This is a phrase you can use when you want to exchange contact information with someone you've become friendly with and want to connect with on social media. Asking for someone's contact information directly can feel a bit intimidating, so by phrasing it this way, you can express your desire to exchange contact information in a more natural way.

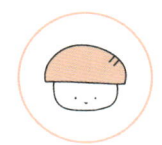

Facebook やっていますか？
フェイスブック

Feisubukku yatte imasu ka?
Do you have a Facebook?

🔊 43-2

いいえ、Facebook は やっていません。
フェイスブック

Iie, feisubukku wa yatte imasen.
No, I don't have a Facebook.

Phrase Practice

Let's try saying the below sentence with the following words inside the parentheses.

（　　　　） やっていますか？
（　　　　） yatte imasu ka?
Do you have a (　　)?

🔊 43-3

ライン	ワッツアップ	エックス	インスタグラム
LINE	**WhatsApp**	**X**	**Instagram**
rain	wattsuappu	ekkusu	insutaguramu

\ Tips / from Tanaka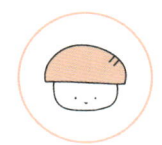

There are more texters than callers in Japan?

In Japan, many people prefer to communicate through text messages rather than phone calls or voice messages. This is because using phones or speaking loudly in places like trains or buses is often considered impolite. Instead, スタンプ (stampu, *stickers*) are commonly used to express feelings that cannot be conveyed through text alone.

PHRASE

44

おめでとうございます。

Omedetoo gozaimasu.
Congratulations.

🔊 44-1

...Soshite dai ichi i wa...
...And first place goes to...

Kirin san desu!!
Kirin-san!

Omedetoo gozaimasu!
Congratulations!

'Yume ka...'
'Just a dream huh...'

This phrase is used to express joy and celebration on happy occasions like birthdays, school admissions, graduations, weddings, and other special events. For instance, leaving a heartfelt comment on your favorite celebrity's social media on their birthday would be a nice use.

108

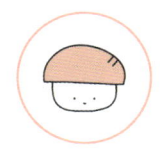

きりんさん、たんじょうび
おめでとうございます！

Kirin san, tanjoobi
omedetoo gozaimasu!
Kirin-san, happy birthday!

Conversation Example

🔊 44-2

ありがとうございます！

Arigatoo gozaimasu!
Thank you!

Phrase Practice

🔊 44-3

Let's try saying the below sentence
with the following words inside the parentheses.

（　　　　）おめでとうございます。
（　　　　）omedetoo gozaimasu.
Congratulations on your (　　).

たんじょうび	そつぎょう	けっこん
tanjoobi	sotsugyoo	kekkon
birthday	*graduation*	*marriage*

\ Tips / from Tanaka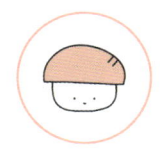

New Year's greetings

One classic phrase using おめでとうございます is あけまして おめでとうございます
(Akemashite omedetoo gozaimasu, *Welcoming this new year*).

This phrase is used as a New Year's greeting, similar to "Happy New Year," to celebrate the arrival of the new year. It's worth noting that while "Happy New Year" can be used before the new year begins, あけまして おめでとうございます is specifically used after the new year has started.

Unique Aspects of Japanese Culture

Here, I'll introduce some aspects of Japanese culture and customs that you might find a little surprising when in Japan.

Lack of Trash Bins in Public Spaces

In Japan, there aren't many trash cans in public places. Convenience stores used to have trash cans outside, but nowadays are mostly found inside the stores. This changed to stop crimes and to prevent people from dumping their household garbage.

Limited Physical Affection

In Japan, compared to many other countries, there is less emphasis on physical affection, or "skinship." When meeting someone for the first time, it's common to bow instead of shaking hands. Even among couples, displays of physical affection such as hugging or kissing in public are not as common as in other countries.

Many People Wearing Masks

Since the outbreak of the novel coronavirus, masks have become widespread worldwide. However, in Japan, wearing masks had already been a common thing. People wear masks not just to prevent the spread of colds or viruses but also to avoid spreading germs when they're feeling under the weather, and even just to hide their faces when they have acne or don't feel like putting on makeup. You'll also see a lot of masks in spring because of hay fever.

Chapter

6

Help
Phrases

さいふを なくしました。

Saifu o nakushimashita.
I lost my wallet.

🔊 45-1

どうしましたか？

Doo shimashita ka?
Is something the matter?

さいふを なくしました

Saifu o nakushimashita.
I lost my wallet.

なかないで。あめどうぞ

Nakanai de. Ame doozo.
Don't cry, now. Have a candy.

わたし 子どもじゃないです！

Watashi kodomo ja nai desu!
I'm not a kid!

You can use this phrase when you have lost something. No matter how careful you are, you'll eventually accidentally lose or forget things. However in Japan, lost items often get returned quite frequently, so don't give up so easily if it happens to you. If you know where you lost it, try to contact whatever facility you lost it in. If you're unsure where you lost it, go to the nearest *koban* (police box) and file a lost property report. If you do this, you'll be contacted if your lost item is found.

どうしましたか？
Doo shimashita ka?
Is something the matter?

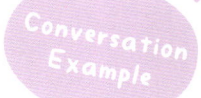

🔊 45-2

スマホを なくしました。
Sumaho o nakushimashita.
I lost my phone.

この かみに なまえを かいてください。
Kono kami ni namae o kaite kudasai.
Please write your name on this paper.

Let's try saying the below sentence
with the following words inside the parentheses.

🔊 45-3

（　　　）を なくしました。
（　　　）o nakushimashita.
I lost my (　　).

スマホ	かばん	ゆびわ
sumaho	kaban	yubiwa
phone	*bag*	*ring*

\ Tips / from Tanaka

When in doubt, go to the *koban*

A *koban* is a type of police box that are widely placed throughout Japan. They play a crucial role in maintaining the safety of local communities by patrolling the area, assisting lost children, and providing assistance to residents in lots of different situations. If you lose something, get lost, or encounter any trouble, it's recommended to visit the nearest *koban* for help.

電車に スマホを わすれました。

でんしゃ

Densha ni sumaho o wasuremashita.

I forgot my phone on the train.

Sumimasen.
Excuse me.

Densha ni sumaho o wasuremashita.
I forgot my phone on the train.

Koko ni denwa bangoo o kaite kudasai.
Please write your phone number here.

Sumaho o minai to wakarimasen.
I need a phone for that.

You can use this phrase to let someone know you left something on the train. If you forget something on the train, contact the railway company or consult with the station staff at the nearest station. The lost and found section at the stations receive lots of items like smartphones, wallets, bags and umbrellas every day. It's a good habit to check your immediate surroundings for forgotten items before getting off the train.

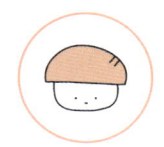

電車に かさを わすれました。
Densha ni kasa o wasuremashita.
I forgot my umbrella on the train.

Conversation Example

🔊 46-2

どんな かさですか？
Donna kasa desu ka?
What does it look like?

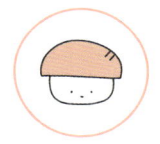

あおい かさです。
Aoi kasa desu.
It's blue.

Phrase Practice

🔊 46-3

Let's try saying the below sentence with the following words inside the parentheses.

電車に（　　　）を わすれました。
Densha ni (　　　) o wasuremashita.
I forgot my (　　　) on the train.

かさ	イヤホン	てぶくろ
kasa	iyahon	tebukuro
umbrella	*earphones*	*gloves*

Other easily forgotten items

さいふ	かばん	かぎ	ハンカチ
saifu	kaban	kagi	hankachi
wallet	*bag*	*key*	*handkerchief*

きぶんが わるいです。

Kibun ga warui desu.

I'm not feeling very well.

Kibun ga warui desu.
I'm not feeling very well.

Sukoshi yasumimashoo.
Let's take a little break.

Aisu o katte kimashita.
I got you ice cream.

Chokoaji ga yokatta desu.
I wish you had gotten chocolate flavor.

You can use this phrase to express that you aren't feeling well. It allows you to communicate that you're not feeling well without specifying particular symptoms like dizziness or nausea, which can be challenging vocabulary-wise. If you start feeling unwell while you're out, don't hesitate to inform those around you about your situation. You should be able to get some assistance, such as being guided to a place where you can sit or lie down for some rest.

エッグさん、だいじょうぶですか？

Eggu san, daijoobu desu ka?

Egg-san, are you alright?

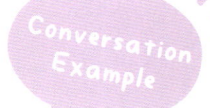 Conversation Example

🔊 47-2

すこし きぶんが わるいです。

Sukoshi kibun ga warui desu.

Actually, I'm not feeling very well.

あそこの ベンチで やすみましょう。

Asoko no benchi de yasumimashoo.

Let's take a break at the bench over there.

 Tips from Tanaka

Be careful of heat stroke in summer

Japan's summer is marked by high temperatures and high humidity. Depending on the region, temperatures can reach upward of nearly 40 degrees Celsius, with humidity levels exceeding 80%. High humidity makes it difficult for sweat to evaporate, which increases the risk of heatstroke. People who are not used to the hot and humid weather, especially those from cooler regions, need to be especially careful. Consider the following measures to prevent heatstroke:

- – Use a parasol or hat to block out the sun.
- – Stay hydrated by drinking plenty of fluids and replenishing electrolytes regularly.
- – Avoid going out during the hottest parts of the day.

If you start feeling unwell due to the heat while you're out, it's advisable to seek refuge in air-conditioned places like shops and take a rest.

あたまが いたいです。

Atama ga itai desu.
My head hurts.

◁» 48-1

エッグさん だいじょうぶですか？

Eggu san daijoobu desu ka?
Egg-san, are you okay?

あたまが いたいです…

Atama ga itai desu...
My head hurts...

ねつが ありますか？

Netsu ga arimasu ka?
Do you have a fever?

やっぱりねつが ありますね

Yappari netsu ga arimasu ne.
I knew it, you do have a fever.

You can use this phrase to communicate that you have a headache or are in pain. It can also be used when describing symptoms at a hospital or pharmacy. On the next page, you will find the names of major parts of the body which you can refer to. If you don't know the name of a painful area, you can also point to the location and say, ここが いたいです (Koko ga itai desu, *This place hurts*).

どこが いたいですか？
Doko ga itai desu ka?
Where does it hurt?

🔊 48-2

あしが いたいです。
Ashi ga itai desu.
My legs hurt.

Phrase Practice

🔊 48-3

Let's try saying the below sentence
with the following words inside the parentheses.

（　　　）が いたいです。
（　　　）ga itai desu.
I have pain in my (　　).

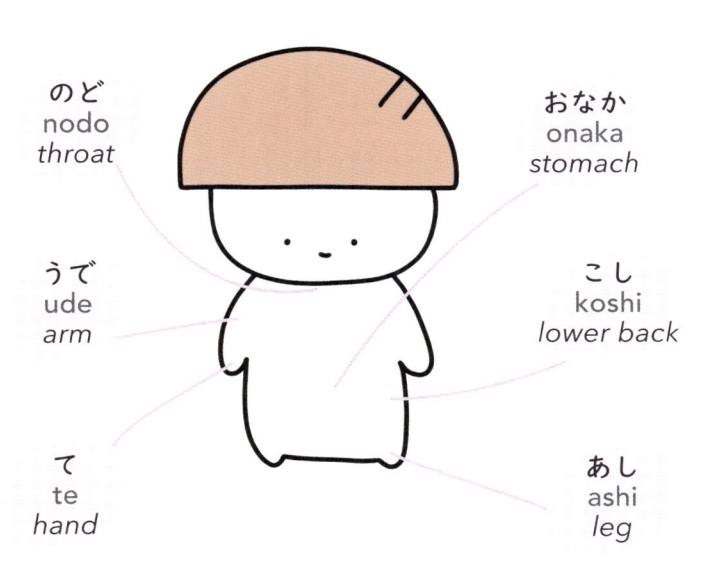

のど
nodo
throat

おなか
onaka
stomach

うで
ude
arm

こし
koshi
lower back

て
te
hand

あし
ashi
leg

すこし よこに なりたいです。

Sukoshi yoko ni naritai desu.
I need to lie down for a little bit.

Daijoobu desu ka?
Are you okay?

Sukoshi yoko ni naritai desu.
I need to lie down for a little bit.

Chigau hoohoo de kaerimashoo.
Let's get home a different way.

Kore wa raku desu ne.
This is easy.

You can use this phrase when you're not feeling well but just need a little rest to recover, or feeling tired but not to the point of needing an ambulance. If after resting you still don't feel well and then need to call an ambulance, you can say きゅうきゅうしゃを よんでください (Kyuukyuusha o yonde kudasai, *Please call an ambulance*). In Japan, the use of ambulances is free, and even foreigners temporarily staying in Japan, such as tourists, don't entail any charges (though medical expenses may apply if treated upon arrival).

どうしましたか？
Doo shimashita ka?
Is there a problem?

🔊 49-2

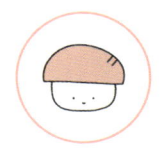

きぶんが わるいです。
すこし よこに なりたいです。
Kibun ga warui desu. Sukoshi yoko ni naritai desu.
I don't feel good. I'd like to lie down for a little bit.

こちらへ どうぞ。
Kochira e doozo.
This way.

 Tips from Tanaka

If you feel sick at the train station

In crowded places like Tokyo, trains can get extremely congested. Especially during weekday mornings and evenings, the rush hour commute can be so packed that there's barely any room to move. Some people, like Tanaka-san in the 4-panel comic, may start to feel unwell in such crowded trains.

If you start feeling unwell on a train, it's important to get off at the nearest station and inform a station attendant. At larger stations, you can often rest in a first aid room if needed, and they can even provide a wheelchair if walking is difficult. Even if you don't ever experience such a situation, knowing that you can seek help if necessary can be reassuring.

PHRASE 50

たすけてください！

Tasukete kudasai!

Somebody help!

🔊 50-1

A...!
Ouch.

Tanaka san!!
Tanaka-san!!

Dareka...
Somebody...
Tasukete kudasai!!
Help!!

Ano... watashi daijoobu desu...
Hey, I'm fine...

You can use this phrase to call for help in emergencies. If there is trouble, it's important not to try to handle it alone and to ask for help from people nearby. Note that this phrase is used in quite urgent situations. For example, in less urgent situations like needing help carrying some luggage, you would use てつだってください (Tetsudatte kudasai) rather than たすけてください. While both situations can be expressed as "help" in English, in Japanese, different words are used, so please just try to keep that in mind.

たすけてください！
Tasukete kudasai!
Somebody help!

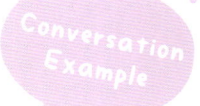

🔊 50-2

どうしましたか？
Doo shimashita ka?
What's wrong?

ともだちが けがを しました。
Tomodachi ga kega o shimashita.
My friend is injured.

Emergency phrases

Bonus Phrases

🔊 50-3

だれか
きてください！
Dareka kite kudasai!
Someone please come!

けいさつを
よんでください！
Keesatsu o yonde kudasai!
Call the police!

きゅうきゅうしゃを
よんでください！
Kyuukyuusha o yonde kudasai!
Call an ambulance!

かじです！
Kaji desu!
There's a fire!

 from Tanaka

Telephone numbers for making emergency calls

The numbers below are emergency phone numbers. It is a good idea to keep these numbers on your phone or in a notebook in case of emergency. There is no charge for emergency calls.

119 : To call the fire department or an ambulance
110 : To call the police

Afterward

Thank you very much for reading this book to the end.

In today's increasingly convenient world where translation apps and AI are so prevalent, it's getting easier and easier to communicate in different languages. You might wonder what the point of learning a language is in such an era. If you believe the sole purpose is just communication, then maybe you're right; maybe there's no longer a need to learn languages.

However, I believe that in such times, it's become even more important to learn the language of others. I believe that it's important to have a communicative attitude, as that is the way to connect deeply with people from different cultures.

When I was a university student, I traveled on my own to about 13 European countries. I crammed in basic phrases in English, and other local languages, and struggled through interactions with locals. But I still vividly remember that sense of joy and accomplishment when I was able to understand what they were saying or when they understood what I was saying.

I wrote this book based on those experiences, hoping that those of you learning Japanese can also experience that same feeling.

I really believe that learning a language opens the door to a new world. I hope this book serves as an entry point for you to become interested in Japanese language and culture, to meet new people, and to touch upon a world you didn't know before.

Finally, I would like to express my sincere gratitude to Kurosio Publishers for providing me with this wonderful opportunity to create this book and for sticking by me this whole time.

Tanaka

おわりに

　本書を最後まで読んでいただき、ありがとうございます。

　翻訳アプリや AI が普及した今の便利な世の中では、異なる言語で簡単にコミュニケーションをとることができます。そのような時代に言語を学ぶことにはどのような意味があるのでしょうか。

　意思疎通することだけが目的なら、もはや言語を学ぶ必要なんてないのかもしれません。

　しかしそのような時代だからこそ、異なる文化を持つ人と深くつながるためには、相手の言語を学び、話そうとする姿勢がより重要なのだと私は考えています。

　私は大学生のとき、ヨーロッパの国々を 13 カ国ほど一人旅しました。

　英語や現地の言語の基本的なフレーズを頭に詰め込み、四苦八苦しながら現地の人と交流しましたが、相手の話したことを理解することができたり、自分の話したことを理解してもらえたりしたときの喜びや達成感を今でも鮮明に覚えています。

　私自身のそのような経験から、日本語を学んでいるみなさんにも同じ気持ちを味わってもらいたいという思いで本書を執筆しました。

　言語を学ぶことは、新しい世界へとつながる扉を開くことだと私は考えています。

　本書がみなさんにとって日本語や日本の文化に興味を持つ入り口となり、新しい人と出会い、これまで知らなかった世界にふれるきっかけとなれば幸いです。

　最後になりましたが、本書を作成する素晴らしい機会をくださり、長い間伴走してくださったくろしお出版の皆様に心より感謝申し上げます。

たなか

Listening to the Audio

You can download the audio package by scanning the code below.

■URL

https://www.9640.jp/books_975/

About the Author

Tanaka
たなか

Learn Japanese
with Tanaka san

Born and raised in Japan, Tanaka has been running a YouTube channel "Learn Japanese with Tanaka san" since 2021 which boasts a subscriber count of 640,000 as of 2025. Her fun Japanese language educational content uses illustrations and animations and is popular with Japanese language learners around the world.

日本生まれ日本育ち。2021年よりYouTubeチャンネル『Learn Japanese with Tanaka san』を運営。イラストやアニメーションを使った楽しい日本語教育コンテンツが世界中の日本語学習者から人気を集め、YouTubeのチャンネル登録者数は64万人以上（2025年3月現在）。

Handy Japanese Conversations
Master Phrases through MANGA

| 初版第1刷 | 2024年9月10日 |
| 第3刷 | 2025年4月15日 |

著　　　者　Tanaka

発　行　人　岡野 秀夫
発　行　所　株式会社くろしお出版
　　　　　　〒102-0084　東京都千代田区二番町4-3
　　　　　　[電話] 03-6261-2867　[WEB] www.9640.jp

印刷・製本　シナノ書籍印刷
ブックデザイン　駒井和彬（こまる図考室）
翻訳協力　Maha & Connor McElligott
音声協力　狩生健志

ご案内